THE LAW OF
ATTRACTION
MADE EASY

More Than
50 EXERCISES
.... TO ....
*Manifest the Life
You Want*

MEERA LESTER

Adams Media
New York London Toronto Sydney New Delhi

Adams Media
An Imprint of Simon & Schuster, Inc.
57 Littlefield Street
Avon, Massachusetts 02322

For information about special discounts for bulk purchases, please contact Simon & Schuster Special Sales at 1-866-506-1949 or business@simonandschuster.com.

The Simon & Schuster Speakers Bureau can bring authors to your live event. For more information or to book an event contact the Simon & Schuster Speakers Bureau at 1-866-248-3049 or visit our website at www.simonspeakers.com.

Manufactured in the United States of America

10 9 8 7 6 5 4

Library of Congress Cataloging-in-Publication Data has been applied for.

ISBN 978-1-4405-9485-4
ISBN 978-1-4405-9486-1 (ebook)

Contains material adapted from *The Everything® Law of Attraction Book* by Meera Lester, copyright © 2008 by Simon & Schuster, Inc., ISBN 978-1-59869-775-9, and *The Everything® Law of Attraction Dream Dictionary* by Cathleen O'Connor, copyright © 2010 by Simon & Schuster, Inc., ISBN 978-1-4405-0466-2.

Contents

PART 3: Finding Happiness . . . 131

Introduction

Have you heard of the Law of Attraction, but aren't sure what it is—or how to use it? The Law of Attraction is a concept of harmonious alignment that allows you to draw the things you desire into your life. No matter what you want, the Law of Attraction can help bring it to you. You may already be familiar with the concept of the law. The popular books and CDs about the Law of Attraction by Esther and Jerry Hicks and Michael Losier, among others, as well as the mega-hit *The Secret* by Rhonda Byrne, have catapulted the ages-old principles of this universal spiritual law into greater public awareness.

Whatever you most desire and think about most often is sure to manifest through the Law of Attraction. You can have whatever you want. You may seek:

- Robust health or longevity
- Some of the finer things in life, such as a sleek car or a lovely piece of jewelry
- The perfect romantic partner
- A well-paying job or a path to a new career
- Spiritual advancement
- Happiness and peace of mind

Those are all perfectly reasonable and attainable goals.

The universal Law of Attraction is always working to produce the experiences, relationships, and things you think about most. If you are worried about breaking a bone, you will likely draw it in and it will happen. Fear attracts more of the thing you fear.

But take heart! The good news is that the reverse is also true. When you desire to manifest money, your desire yoked with feelings of excited anticipation can bring you financial prosperity. You can shift your thoughts to bring more positive and happy experiences, and through transformational thinking, you can radically change your life. And it doesn't stop there. When you team up harmoniously with the Law of Attraction and with other like-minded people, you can work together to bring about change in the world. You and everyone who is deliberately working with the Law of Attraction become co-creators with the Divine through the power of your heart and mind.

These steps are not difficult steps to master. Use this book to become informed, inspired, and confident as you begin to work with the Law of Attraction. With more than 50 easy-to-implement exercises, you will soon be engaged in the transformational thinking that brings about exciting and positive changes in your life!

PART 1

The Law of Attraction Basics

Some people have called the Law of Attraction a recently discovered ancient secret teaching. Indeed, the law is ancient in its origins. Whether or not it was ever lost or purposefully kept secret is arguable. What is true is that through the centuries, various spiritual teachers, philosophers, and others have mentioned or discussed the Law of Attraction, although they used various other names in their teachings and writings. Today, renewed interest in the subject has catapulted the ages-old concept into mainstream popular culture while simultaneously placing it under a lens of scrutiny.

CHAPTER 1

What Is the Law of Attraction?

WHAT THE LAW IS AND ISN'T

Simply put, the Law of Attraction asserts that a person's thoughts attract objects, people, and situations and circumstances, both positive and negative, into his life. You've heard old adages such as "like attracts like," "birds of a feather flock together," "as above, so below," "what you send out comes back multiplied many times over," and "ask and ye shall receive." Consider these, and you have an idea of what the Law of Attraction is.

ATTRACTION CAN BRING WHAT YOU DO—OR DON'T—WANT

Proponents of the Law of Attraction say that the law brings you whatever you think about most. Thoughts can become emotionally charged. When you desire something—say, a new outfit—you feel emotion each time your mind thinks about having that new dress, jacket, shoes, and handbag. You are filled with excitement at the possibility of having your desire fulfilled. You believe you can have it. You deserve it. It is coming. You consider ways to speed up getting that outfit. You might even develop a plan of action for getting the money to go shopping at the mall. Consider the following example, a true story.

Evidence of the Law of Attraction

During a recent move from Illinois to Missouri, a single mother inadvertently left behind her favorite cast iron skillet. Each day she thought of that old skillet in which she could cook anything, even a cake. She obsessed about getting another one and even asked for it in her prayers. Throughout the day, she thought about how much she would enjoy cooking again once she got her new skillet. She knew that a cast iron skillet was not too expensive, but her financial resources were limited and she would have to budget carefully. Whenever she thought about having the skillet, she felt happy and joyful. At the end of the month, however, after she had paid all her bills, there was not enough money left over to make her purchase. Undaunted, the mother reaffirmed her goal to save a little whenever and however she could in order to get her skillet.

A few months after her move, the young mother met an elderly gentleman carrying a box of discarded kitchen items from a nearby apartment to the dumpster. On top of the box was a cast iron skillet. The woman inquired of the man whether he was throwing it away. When he told her he was, she asked if she could have it. He gave it to her. Overcome with gratitude, the young mother thanked the man again and again.

How did this come to pass?

Her fixation on having the skillet brought it to her, and she did not have to purchase it. If she had felt an abiding desperation that she was doomed to always be poor and never have the basic necessities, her fears would have manifested that lack. Her thoughts of poverty would have brought more lack in her life rather than the skillet she desired.

A thorough understanding of the fundamentals of the Law of Attraction allows you to quickly achieve your goals, get more of what you want, and avoid attracting what you do not want. With deliberate and focused application of the principles of the Law of Attraction, we can all achieve our full human potential and work together toward creating a more harmonious and just world.

Where the Law Came From

According to some who have studied it, the universal great Law of Attraction has been with us since the beginning of time, perhaps even at the moment of creation and the beginning of thought. Others say it is impossible to pinpoint exactly when the concept entered human consciousness.

IN THE BEGINNING

Some people say that the entire universe and our world were first conceived in the mind of our Creator, then were manifested through the creative energies of the universe out of the realms of infinite potential and substance. Further, they suggest that God created humans as sentient beings with minds that could also imagine and create. New Age spiritual seekers refer to the Creator as Divine Mind, the Universe, the Source, and many other names. For those with a more traditional viewpoint, the Creator is God. Genesis, the first book of the Bible, sets forth the creation story, which begins in the mind of God. With His intention and declaration, heaven and earth and everything therein were formed.

ANCIENT POSSIBILITIES

Some self-help experts say the Law of Attraction possibly dates as far back as 6,000 to 7,000 years ago, where it found expression in the mystical traditions and beliefs of the ancients. Magicians of long ago certainly observed and wrote about affinities between things before the advent of science. Translations of ancient texts suggest that our spiritual ancestors thought a lot about the heaven and earth and pondered the relationships between things. The Emerald Tablet of Hermes, whose date of origin is uncertain, contains verses by Hermes, purportedly an Egyptian sage. His verses assert that all things in the world are interconnected and that thoughts impact things. The tablet contains the verse that has been translated to become the well-known adage "as above, so below."

A Creator by Any Other Name

The Creator has been called by myriad names, including God, Divine Mind, Divine Intelligence, Elohim, Holy One, Yahweh, Powers that Be, Abba, Divine Father, Divine Mother, Universe, Source, Allah, Friend, Maker, Primordial Consciousness, Everlasting Lord, Supreme Being, Alpha and the Omega, Ishvara, and the Beloved.

WATTLES AND PEALE

Others say the Law of Attraction concept is decidedly more modern and is possibly just an updated version of the teachings of the late Wallace D. Wattles (1860–1911) and Dr. Norman Vincent Peale (1898–1993). Wattles, who was born into poverty and became wealthy, wrote about the science of getting rich. Peale became famous for his ideas about the power of positive thinking. Both men emphasized the role of conscious and intensely focused thought in achieving the desired goal. Both men believed in a higher power at work in human lives. Wattles referred to it as "formless" intelligence and substance.

Norman Vincent Peale, author of *The Power of Positive Thinking*, a popular self-help guide first published in 1952, advocated that people trust that God's higher power was always with them. He observed that when they affirmed, visualized, and believed that God's power was at work in their lives, they energized their belief, actualized that power, and achieved astonishing results.

Peale, a clergyman, spoke and wrote of the power and presence of God. Today many people believe that a divine consciousness permeates the universe and that when they align themselves in harmony with that consciousness, they become co-creators of their destinies with the Divine. Individuals can tap into the realm of infinite potential and substance. Through their thoughts, they draw into their lives all circumstances, situations, relationships, experiences, and things. The process is continuous and unending.

FUNDAMENTALS OF THE LAW

The Law of Attraction works in response to thoughts that have become energized. What if you deliberately focused your attention on something that you wanted to call forth in your life, something you deeply desired to manifest? Would the Law of Attraction bring it to you? The answer is yes. Always.

HOW DOES IT WORK?

Proponents of the Law of Attraction assert that the law brings you what you desire when you:

1. Are clear about what you want
2. Energize your desire for the item with thoughts, emotion, visual imagery, and a strong conviction that it is coming to you
3. Feel and express gratitude for what you already have and that which you desire, even if it has not yet come into your experience

The Law of Attraction is not wishful thinking, daydreaming, or a momentary flight of fancy. If the young mother had simply wished for the skillet, it is unlikely that the skillet would have shown up in her life. A wish is not a strong enough intention. The law is always working to give people the very things they most desire.

At first it may seem impossible that a person could shrink his debt, acquire wealth, and grow that wealth as much as his mind could imagine. But the Law of Attraction makes anything possible. There are myriad resources to teach individuals how to get rich. Often such books offer advice about how to assess your indebtedness, develop a financial plan, imagine putting every step of the plan in place, visualize what's going to happen, and actualize the events. In this way, the person accelerates the working of the Law of Attraction.

Some experts on the Law of Attraction have pointed out that as soon as someone begins focusing on the thing he really wants, the universe gets busy arranging or rearranging the necessary elements and circumstances to make manifestation of that thing possible. The process can be accelerated with a little planning. A debt-free life, new friends, a loving life partner, plenty of money, a new car, or a dream job—whatever the person desires will manifest. When someone decides to accelerate the process and works out a plan to allow for that manifestation, myriad opportunities begin to present themselves. A person working with the Law of Attraction need only change his mindset and be aware that the opportunities for manifestation of his desire will become more commonplace. It is as if the universe is working with you, putting wind in the sail of your dream ship to take you anywhere you want to go and give you the experiences, relationships, money, wealth, and things you most desire.

DELIBERATE INTENTION TAKES FOCUS

Think of how something looks under a magnifying glass or a microscope. The subject being studied comes into crisp focus and is magnified many times. This is what you do when you work with the Law of Attraction. With deliberate intention, your thoughts necessarily become not only highly focused but more concentrated and energized. You must have the intent of receiving what you wish for and not waver in your belief that the manifestation is already in the works. Dream what may have been impossible for you before you knew about the Law of Attraction. Now you understand that anything you desire will be possible to achieve or obtain. The Law of Attraction is continually responding to whatever you are thinking and feeling. Contemplate all things related to the object or circumstance that you seek to manifest. Wrap your thoughts around your desire, sharpen your focus, and feel expectant to draw the desired object to you.

The Power of Your Brain

The most powerful tool you have for creating is your brain, or more precisely, a particular area of your brain. According to ScienceDaily.com, the brain's "default network" enables you to do introspective tasks. Because of this you can construct a self-narrative of your life story—crucial for imagining changes to it—and mentalize or analyze another's mental state so that you can appropriately adjust your own, which is important for developing relationships.

Just as your thoughts can attract things you want, they can also attract things you do *not* want. Whatever you fear most and think about often or obsessively can also manifest itself in your life.

For example, you may love hiking around the Mojave Desert, but your greatest fear is that someday you'll encounter a rattlesnake that you didn't see until you were right upon it. You've thought about how terrified you would be when the snake strikes at your leg or foot. Repetitive thoughts that are charged with fear can set up the experience unless you let go of it. It is better to banish such dark thoughts. Don't give up hiking in the desert, though. Instead, be measured, thoughtful, studied, and prudent about undertaking such a hike. Know what precautions to take in order to have a safe hike. Replace your fearful thoughts with a sure-fire belief in a higher power working through you and with you and at all times ensuring your safety.

Careless thinking about negative events (like the snake in the desert) can just as easily draw similar negative experiences into your life. Most likely you'll protest and declare that you would never want those things to happen; you would never have deliberately drawn them to you. But when you begin to correlate your thinking with events that have happened or that are occurring in your life, you will begin to see how your thoughts influence your life experiences.

ANYONE CAN USE THE LAW

Anyone can work with the Law of Attraction to deliberately make choices about what she wants and doesn't want in her life. She can use the law to help her work out her dreams, desires, and ambitions. So, too, she can repel the things she does not want. Worries about debt, for example, can bring more debt. But when thoughts of poverty are replaced by images of abundance, the Law of Attraction springs into action to replace lack with abundance.

That's right: Anyone can use the Law of Attraction to change her financial status or anything else she desires. You can have the kind of life you choose. It just takes a little imagination. Whether it is dreaming or awake, the mind thinks in images and symbols. Proponents of the Law of Attraction say that when you can clearly imagine having what you most want, the Law of Attraction takes over and gives it to you.

THE LAW IS UNBIASED

The Law of Attraction does not judge the value or worth of your thoughts. It doesn't care whether they are harmful or well intentioned, nor does it value whether your thoughts arise from a particular belief system. You may eschew religion and be an atheist or agnostic, or you may be deeply religious. Knowledge and practice of a spiritual tradition (or lack of belief) doesn't concern the working of the law. What matters is how you feel about what you are thinking.

Gratitude plays a role because of how it makes you feel. For example, when you are grateful for having something, you feel good and the thoughts of possession and the positive feelings of possession bring more of the same. The law always responds to what you focus on in your thoughts and the emotion you generate in response to those thoughts; feeling strengthens the attracting power of thought.

Thinking good thoughts instead of dark or evil ones is a way of doing good. When you silently bless others, that is a good thing and good is attracted back into your life. You've no doubt heard the phrase "What goes around comes around." It comes back to magnetic attraction. When you pray and do good deeds—acts of kindness such as putting money in a stranger's expired parking meter—your thoughts and actions bear the fruit of goodness. Consider for a moment what kinds of thoughts and feelings, mental images, words, and deeds you are sending out. What is in your life that you don't like? What would you change? What do you desire?

If you think you are doing everything correctly to manifest your desires but they haven't come to you yet, perhaps you need to clear some clutter and make a space for it—in other words, create a vacuum.

THE LAW WORKS WHEN THERE IS A VACUUM

If someone wants to manifest something in his work or life experience, he may first have to create the space for it. In other words, he must tear down, remove, and otherwise clean and clear a space to make it ready to receive the object or create the right climate for getting a new job, raise in pay, loving companion, or group of friends. The ancient Chinese tradition of feng shui emphasizes the clearing of space and the art of placement to attract the things you desire in your life. Clutter impedes or blocks energy flow. When you are trying to bring something good into your life, you certainly don't want to block its arrival. You can use the principles of feng shui to enhance your intentional work with the Law of Attraction, especially if you are seeking harmony, peace, and prosperity in all areas of your life. One of the major maxims of feng shui states that "Less is more."

SEEING BLOCKAGES

A woman whose freelance writing career seemed stalled decided to consult a feng shui expert who understood the Law of Attraction. A cursory examination of the writer's home office revealed multiple problems with the space. Her plants were dying. Dust-covered books filled bookcases, some in precarious stacks that threatened to topple off if they were bumped. The partially open drawers of the file cabinet revealed the need for a vigorous pruning of outdated files. Multiple calendars, a photocopied page of editing marks, and other pieces of paper with notes that had been tacked above the desk overpowered the framed art on the walls. The room was cluttered and unwelcoming. The writer complained of lack of money and writing jobs. Her life, she said, like her office, seemed to be spiraling out of control. She wanted to attract better assignments for more money.

The consultant first asked the writer to clarify what she wanted. She also asked the writer to be clear about what she didn't want in her business life. Then she had the writer clear and clean the space. She suggested to the writer that she throw out the dead plants and box up some of the books for storage. The rest fit in neat rows on the shelves. She recommended bringing in a thriving money plant, a beautiful orchid, and a small desktop fountain to shift the energies in the office.

The writer was encouraged to become more organized. Her organization efforts meant she became more productive and had more time to pursue new project ideas. The newly cleaned and well-organized space inspired the writer to be more creative. She began to spend a few minutes each day visualizing the kinds of projects she wanted and the amount of money she desired for each. When new writing assignments started flowing in, the writer saw for herself why creating a vacuum for the work she desired had been necessary.

When you open the space in your life to manifest something, the substance of the universe will fill it, according to Catherine Ponder, author of *The Dynamic Laws of Prosperity*. Test the Law of Attraction for yourself. If you are experiencing lack when you seek abundance, look first to your thoughts. Are they positive? Have you unwittingly created any blockages? If so, remove them. Create a vacuum for what you want. Riches, expensive jewelry, a new house, a hot car, a super-healthy body, a new boyfriend, spiritual insights, weight loss, or even a business of your own—you can have whatever you want. That's the promise of the law when you work deliberately with it.

Ten Ways to Use the Law of Attraction to Get Everything Your Heart Desires

When you have an understanding of what the law of attraction is, you can begin to dream big. Here are just ten ways the law of attraction can change your life.

1. Release fear and self-limiting thoughts and start believing in the power of the universe to allow your boldest dreams to manifest.

2. Achieve unbelievable success in your chosen career path, even if it has previously eluded you.

3. Gain mastery over your life and learn to live in harmony with your spiritual destiny.

4. Draw financial prosperity into your life and grow your wealth.

5. Fearlessly follow your passion to produce and market your gifts to the world.

6. Enhance the value and meaning of your life and your endeavors.

7. Attract the perfect romantic partner and other helpful people into your life.

8. Understand the universal spiritual laws of success and how to apply them to gain your deepest desires.

9. Advance faster upon your chosen spiritual path and gain greater insight and wisdom into the secrets of the universe.

10. Discover transformational thinking to change your life, and align with like-minded people to effect positive change locally, nationally, or globally.

You'll find specific tips for realizing these intentions in Part 2.

CHAPTER 2

How to Use the Law of Attraction

THE BUILDING BLOCK OF THE UNIVERSE

Many practitioners of the Law of Attraction have noted that the interrelationship between thoughts and things is dependent on the psychic energy generated by creative thought. Such energized thought sets up the attraction. Just as the mind can use the power of creative and positive thought to attract things, such as healing in the body, it can also attract objects and situations it desires through thought energy.

Who Discovered Psychic Energy?

Psychic energy was a concept first developed by a German named Ernst von Brücke, whose ideas influenced Sigmund Freud and later Freud's student, the noted psychologist Carl Jung. Their work and writings put forth the idea that humans emanated a mental or psychic energy that could be detected and that was used in certain psychological activities.

Atoms are the building blocks of matter, while energy has been called the workhorse of creation. From grade-school science, you may have learned that the energy of the universe can change from one form to another, seem to disappear, move about, or remain available as potential energy. You probably also learned about the two main categories of energy:

1. Kinetic, or energy in motion
2. Potential, or energy that is stored or in position to be released

Both energy types have relevance to the Law of Attraction. Energy is what enables the work of the entire universe to get done, whether the work is fueling the tasks of creation or simply digesting food or thinking thoughts. When you eat a meal, your body receives energy from the food it has digested. It stores excess calories to be accessed later. Energy of one type can change or be converted into a different type. For example, electric energy becomes magnetic when it is run through an electromagnet. But what kind of energy is associated with our thoughts? That's a difficult question to answer, although some insight can be gained by shifting our lens from empirical science to esoteric and metaphysical ideas found in Eastern philosophy.

THOUGHTS ARE THINGS

Some people believe that our lives express our interior worlds, or what we think about. You might have heard the saying that "thoughts are things." In fact, in Hinduism, nothing exists apart from the Divine because it permeates all things.

Although it is invisible to the naked eye, energy may be perceived and felt. It's been said that you can't fool kids or dogs because they have a natural ability to sense whether someone's energy and intention toward them are good or bad. Certain psychics, mediums, and empathic people possess a heightened sensitivity to the electromagnetic energy that is retained in objects, haunted houses, sacred places, crime scenes, and the like. Psychic energy lives on in those objects and places.

Even as doctors work in integrative medicine, using both Western and Eastern medical knowledge, and high-performance sports experts counsel their athletes about an intrinsic mind/body connection, scientific research continues on the subject of thoughts as energy.

Energy, Around the World

While some skeptics doubt that consciousness and human thought has any measurable energy, others, including spiritual seekers, scientists, practitioners of Eastern religions, and philosophers, disagree. Indeed, some people believe human consciousness itself may be energy.

SHAKTI

In India, modern spiritual seekers make pilgrimages to the sacred places associated with holy people of the past because the shakti (divine energy or holy psychic energy) of those beings remains in the places where those saints prayed, meditated, and became enlightened. Many modern spiritual seekers further believe that the energy stored in sacred places has a beneficial effect on their spiritual efforts to attain enlightenment. Contact with the shakti of enlightened beings, although those saints no longer live in human form, could awaken the Kundalini Shakti. This is the innate and essential divine energy that leads human consciousness to union with God (or absolute divine consciousness) as the energy makes its ascent from the base of the spine to the energy center located on top of the head. The modern seeker's thought, magnetized by her spiritual desire for enlightenment, could manifest her desire, making her thought become the thing she most ardently seeks and desires.

PRANA

Pranic energy represents a kind of bridge between thoughts becoming or manifesting as things. In ancient Hindu writings, the body's vital airs or energies were referred to as prana. Pranic energy permeates all things, including the human mind (and, thus, thought), according to the Hindu sacred scriptures known as the Upanishads. Those sacred writings associate prana ("breath" in Sanskrit) with vitality, and express the idea that a person's prana survives throughout eternity or until a being's soul reincarnates. Prana, often mistakenly thought of as breath, is more correctly understood as a life-sustaining force. Prana underlies and sustains the universe, according to Hindu belief. Prana, therefore, is found in thoughts, and also material objects. The pranic energy of one human, for example, directed toward another person or object can trigger a response, reaction, or change. Even an energized or magnetized thought can instantly or eventually become the thing that the psychic energy of the creative mind conceives, giving rise to the New Age idea that "thoughts are things."

Current Research Into Human Consciousness

The University of Arizona's Center for Consciousness Studies is one of a number of educational centers, associations, and organizations currently studying various aspects of human consciousness. For more information, see the website *www.consciousness.arizona.edu/mission.htm*.

CHI

The Chinese use the word chi (pronounced *chee*) to mean the natural, supernatural, and spiritual energy of the physical universe and the human body and mind. An imbalance of chi in a person's body or life brings disharmony and disease upon him. Practitioners of acupuncture, chi gong, and other disciplines embrace the concept of chi as a subtle force underlying and permeating all things (like prana). They say restoring the balance of the flow of the chi is what restores balance, health, and harmony. When balance is restored, the things a person desires become manifest through his thought energy.

SUBTLE ENERGIES AND HEALING

Aura healing, chakra healing, reiki (pronounced *RAY kee*), quantum touch, and no-touch healing are all examples of alternative medicine/belief systems that suggest that the vital energy of the body, whether it is called prana, chi, ki, or life force, can be manipulated. Skeptics classify such healings as faith healing and say that if it works at all it is due to the thoughts of the patient, or the placebo effect—that is, the patient believes something is being done to help her feel better, she hopes she will feel better, and subsequently she does. Some might say that the placebo effect causes changes in the patient's neurochemistry that might, in part, explain the healing she received.

Polarity of Thought Energy

Thought, as most Law of Attraction experts point out, is associated with two elements:

1. Content (what the thought is about)
2. Energy (of varying intensity, from weak to strong)

Your thought energy has a polarity that flows either inward or outward. If it is stationary, then it lacks any momentum to carry your intention inward or outward. Intention, or your desire for something, requires energy and polarity to manifest that desire.

Some Law of Attraction teachers have explained the outward and inward polarities of thought energy as follows:

- **Outward polarity** requires an action of giving something to the universe
- **Inward polarity** requires a receptive state in which you receive something from the universe

Understanding the concept is vital to putting the Law of Attraction to work in a deliberate way in your life.

If you need healing from a chronic illness or seek spiritual unfolding, you will focus your thought energy or polarity inward, whereas if you desire a new house or car, you'll focus the polarity outward. Another way to think of it is that when the energy is polarized outward, you become engaged in some action—you create or do something. When the polarity is turned inward, you acquire or become the recipient of something.

Polarity Therapy

Randolph Stone, an Austrian immigrant, combined his lifelong interest in spiritualism and medicine when he formulated the concept that polarized fields of attraction and repulsion exist in all of nature, including the human body. He subsequently developed a holistic treatment for many maladies and called it polarity therapy.

If you have the desire and intention to launch a business, write a screenplay, build a bridge, invent a better mousetrap, or establish a women's collective in a developing country, those thoughts have an outward polarity. The thing you hope to manifest is not so much for you as it is an outward expression of something you wish to do or accomplish. Other examples of outward polarity might include creating a beautiful concrete statue and covering it with mosaics for your local community park, establishing an oral history program that links children with senior citizens in your town, or starting a new nonprofit venture. Think of these manifestations as your gift to the universe.

POSITIVE OR NEGATIVE ATTRACTION

Inherent in the Law of Attraction is the power to attract and repel. Just as batteries have poles that are positive and negative and function to attract and repel, your thoughts also have that power. Have you ever met people who were so self-focused that they seemed to derive pleasure from dwelling on all the things that were going wrong in their lives? They couldn't seem to quit talking about their woes. And you would listen and agree that things seemed pretty bad for them.

Perhaps you wondered what was wrong with that person whose life had enough problems to last several lifetimes. His outer life may simply be a reflection of his interior world. Knowingly or unwittingly, that person is attracting more of what he is thinking about most. And most likely, he is dwelling on everything that could go wrong or get worse.

Continued Negative Thoughts Can Impact Your Life

It's unlikely that you would attract into your life the parallel of an *isolated* thought about something frightening. However, the more often you experience the fear and allow it to build around a specific idea or image, the more likely you are to attract it.

Our thoughts can lift us to joyful heights or cause us to sink into the depths of despair. When we think positively, we bring or attract positive situations and people. But when we focus on the negative aspects of our life, we attract more negativity. Our thoughts are often charged with positive or negative emotion, and are rarely neutral.

If you want more goodness in your life, be good and be grateful. Feel joy and peace and happiness. Spread it out into the universe as your gift to others. Keep your mind clean from clutter, worry, and fear. Don't give mental energy to negative thinking. Just let it go. Focus on the positive to draw more of that into your life.

Conscious and Unconscious Manifesting

Like attracts like. That sums up how the Law of Attraction works. It is not possible for the law to be biased. If you are a happy, upbeat person with a smile for everyone, expect to find friends and good experiences wherever you go. Your thoughts bring those experiences into your life. On the other hand, if you have a negative attitude, a sour expression, and complaints about everything (including each ache and pain in your body), do not be surprised if people avoid you and disease, disaster, and disappointment seem to lurk around every corner.

The Six Basic Steps of Manifesting

To get started with the work of bringing the various circumstances and things that you desire into your life experience, read and practice the following steps. Each is simple and easy to do whenever you have a quiet moment during the day.

1. Clear the clutter, confusion, and negativity from your mind. Try deep breathing, meditation, or quiet reflection to release any doubt, conflicting ideas, or disbelief. Be calmly but intensely focused on the thing you desire to manifest.

2. Set forth the intention to manifest something. Make a mental declaration of your intent. No fuzzy thinking and weak, wishy-washy

dreaming allowed. Be bold and let your mind wrap around the possibility that the thing you most want is already allocated to you by the abundant universe. Perhaps what is coming is even bigger, better, and more beautiful than your desire. Allow for that in your life.

3. Be expectant. Be ready to receive. Believe you deserve it, and that it is already yours.

4. Visualize yourself having it. Feel the emotion associated with getting what you desired. Resist the temptation to question or concern yourself with how the universe rearranges itself to allow your desire to manifest. In other words, don't worry about or question the "how" aspect of manifestation. This is where you suspend disbelief.

5. Feel and express gratitude for the blessings you already have, the gifts of the universe that the higher power makes available to you, and the power that makes each manifestation possible.

6. Repeat these steps often each day. If you skip a day or two of focused thinking about your intention, your desire is still there. Over time the thought energy around your intention may weaken, but if the desire is still strong, the object, situation, or relationship can still come into your life; it simply may take longer to manifest.

You can ramp up the energy of your thought, turning it into a high-energy idea or concept, just as you can build muscle in your body. It just takes practice and frequent repetition. There are many other things you can do as well to intensify the energy about your intention.

INTENSIFY DESIRE AND INTENTION THROUGH SYMBOLISM

In Jungian psychology, symbolism has always served as an important and powerful tool, especially in the healing process. Patients are often encouraged to focus on symbols that embody special meaning for them. These symbols may appear in patients' dreams or in their mindless scribbles and doodles. Those symbols deemed most potent may become departure points or pathways into the psyche.

Use a specific symbol that holds cultural or spiritual meaning for you. Use the symbol throughout the day and also at bedtime as a reminder to meditate or visualize having the thing you most desire. Place the image on a refrigerator, bathroom mirror, or bedside table where it can be easily seen.

USE A SYMBOL TO REPRESENT
TRANSCENDENTAL CONSCIOUSNESS

Symbols have the power to alter consciousness. For example, perhaps you want to use a symbol to represent a metaphysical truth or a transcendent state of mind. The yin/yang symbol that represents the opposite principles of masculine and feminine in Chinese philosophy means harmony, balance, and universal fellowship. A dragon or bear image suggests strength and fortitude.

There are literally thousands of symbols, from ancient to modern. Some may have obscure meanings; others are universally understood. While certain symbols may be associated with myths and cultural traditions, others hold special meaning only for certain groups. The following list contains a few common symbols and colors with their popular meanings:

- Bat: darkness, the unknown
- Blue: sanctity, peace, and water
- Coin: money, wealth, offering
- Diamond: strength, endurance
- Dove: the Holy Spirit, peace
- Full moon: wholeness, completion
- Grove of trees/forest: the unconscious mind; chaos
- Heart: compassion and love
- Lingam: fertility and regeneration
- Ouroboros (snake swallowing its tail): complete cycle of birth, death, and rebirth in an endless round
- Pearl: secret knowledge, hidden truth, wisdom
- Rainbow: a bridge between heaven and earth
- Red: life force, anger, war, Christ's passion

- Snake: deception, sexuality
- Sun: success
- Three: the Holy Trinity; birth, life, and death; past, present, and future
- Two: balance
- Valley: feminine symbol; also death and the unknown
- Violet: sorrow, mysticism
- Volcano/tower: destructive energy

Some symbols have represented a specific meaning for centuries. Symbols such as a wheel, rose, key, cross, and lotus still represent a mystical entry into transcendental states of consciousness and hidden knowledge or wisdom. However, such symbols may also have other meanings associated with them, depending upon the culture in which they are found. For example, the cross, a sacred symbol for Christians, is also the symbol of earth to the Chinese.

FIND A POTENT SYMBOL WITH PERSONAL MEANING

Perhaps you've always wanted a red Porsche convertible. If you find a picture of a red Porsche convertible in a magazine, cut it out and hang it up somewhere. The magazine picture will be a good reminder for you to work with the Law of Attraction to manifest it.

The same is true if you have a recurring dream about, say, searching for a key while climbing to the top of a mountain. Such a dream might be pointing to a search for the key to wisdom and higher states of consciousness as represented by the mountain. It could also mean the challenges you have faced to reach the top.

You may find a powerful symbol in your dreams to use as a touchstone for your work of conscious manifestation. Working with your dreams can be fun, intriguing, and instructive. To discover meanings of symbols that may be appearing in your dreams and also in your conscious waking thoughts, check out David Fontana's book *The Secret Language of Symbols*, Barbara Walker's *The Woman's Dictionary of Symbols and Sacred Objects*, or any of the numerous Internet sites devoted to symbolism.

CHAPTER 3

Myths and Criticisms
of the Law

Is the Law an Overstated Promise?

At best, detractors say, the Law of Attraction overstates a promise that just thinking about something brings it to you. Further, critics argue, you cannot have irrefutable proof of the nonscientific claim that you can gain whatever you dream about or long for—it is not a hypothesis that can be proven through scientific method. Instead, they point out, savvy marketing, attention-grabbing buzzwords, catchy phrases, and the promise of getting something for (almost) nothing seem to have caught the imagination of Americans and the media.

The disenfranchised, poor, aged, infirm, and gullible, critics say, have always been targets for schemes that claim to make their lives easier. When thoughts about great wealth, a Bentley, or a miracle cure don't materialize, disappointment doesn't begin to describe the feelings of the person who had believed in the promise of the Law of Attraction. Yet believers of the law have faith that it is always working to bring the fruits of your thinking into your life.

Infinite Potential for the Many—or Just for a Few?

Law of Attraction teachers and coaches say the law is always working and once you know how to work deliberately with it, you can draw whatever you want from the storehouse of the universe. You have the potential to manifest $1 or $1 million. You could establish a hospital, fund an orphanage, or build a social club for senior citizens. Anything you want to create is possible, provided you have desire, intention, and persistence. You already have the means—your thoughts—assert proponents of the law. Your potential for manifesting is limitless.

Detractors say that the potential to acquire money and material things exists for a few but not everyone, and that money is to be made by those who know how to capitalize on the Law of Attraction. Those who can create a product like the bestselling books and DVDs or become personal coaches, seminar leaders, and lecturers are cashing in on a pop culture phenomenon. Critics add that like most trends, interest will diminish or die out altogether.

Proponents of the Law of Attraction argue that people can create their lives on purpose. In every age and era, there are those who form a strong desire to do something important or meaningful with their lives. In some cases, the desire is simply to build a better mousetrap. In others, it's to give something back to the universe or to do something for the greater social good. Those individuals believe so strongly in what they want that they think about it all the time, perhaps even praying about it and seeking help from the highest Source.

Danger for Desperate People

Critics of the Law of Attraction ask why the Law of Attraction doesn't work for everyone, even those trying their best to work with it. For example, a young man with a family had been busy building his business while also helping his aging father and mother financially. One day, he took ill with a virus that settled in his heart. As he grew weaker, doctors did many tests and finally told him he needed a heart transplant. The young man remained optimistic and followed his doctor's orders but also took up yoga and meditation to draw healing energies into his body.

When it came time for the transplant, he was ready. He was certain that the power of positive thinking could prepare his body for a rapid and complete recovery. He listened to self-healing tapes and did yoga for stress reduction and relaxation. He even had his wife read him a Buddhist prayer each evening to help him visualize perfection in his body and the universe. He felt certain his health would be restored and he would continue doing the work he loved.

The surgery was successful. Elated, the young man and his wife shared his story with others they had met who were facing dire circumstances. Christmas came and went, and the couple looked forward to going dancing on New Year's Eve. The young man was much stronger and had supreme confidence in his new heart. He celebrated the holiday with prayers for the gift of the new heart and for blessings on the donor's family and his own.

On New Year's morning, he awoke with a fever. Two months later, he passed away from an aggressive cancer that had quickly spread throughout his body because his immune system was suppressed. His wife had been more prepared for his death before the transplant. After her husband had received his new heart, she had dared to dream again of their life together, more children, and travels to exotic lands. His death from cancer shocked her.

Although the mind/body connection is still being studied, detractors of the Law of Attraction say the law represents a danger to people in desperate situations. The young man had sought help from alternative therapies and had followed all his doctor's orders. He had followed a course of positive thinking, and yet it had not saved his life. Skeptics say that it is a fallacy to believe that thoughts about having good health can bring about a cure. When, they ask, did wishful or magical thinking ever bestow life for the terminally ill? Yet believers in the working of the law might argue that no one knows what really goes in on in another's mind, what kind of doubts creep in, what kind of fear might be present.

Believers in the Law of Attraction argue that miracle cures, which doctors and science cannot explain, do, in fact, occur. They assert that it is nothing short of arrogant for us to believe that we humans know everything and that the power of healing isn't possible without drugs and medical treatments. People in dire situations often feel helpless and want to do something. Encouraging them to have positive thoughts and focus on the best-case scenario certainly offers a better option than dwelling on the worst-case scenario.

BLAMING THE VICTIMS

According to its proponents, the Law of Attraction mirrors your interior world, manifesting your thoughts in your life experience. The law is always working whether you are conscious of it or not. This idea, argue the law's critics, suggests that a person who has been a victim of adverse circumstances has brought calamity upon herself. Whether she fell prey to identity theft, was laid off or recently fired from her job, or was attacked by a bobcat while running on a woodland trail, she became a victim. Critics assert that Law of Attraction believers fault the individual for such misfortunes. How, skeptics ask, does an unsuspecting person draw such calamity upon herself?

RANDOM ACTS OF VIOLENCE

A young woman crossing her college campus at night became the victim of a man, high on drugs, who physically and sexually assaulted her. The woman lay in a coma for a month before recovering. She was so traumatized that she could not face returning to the school, so she moved across the country and began her life anew. Those who believe in the Law of Attraction might suggest that her thoughts attracted the incident. Others, who believe in reincarnation, might suggest that her attack somehow represented the fruit of a seed planted in previous life. But critics of the Law of Attraction ask how could anyone say to the young woman, "Why did you do that to yourself?"

REPLACE THE NEGATIVE

A woman developed a mass in her breast. Doctors performed various tests, including an x-ray and an ultrasound. Believing the best course was to remove it, they scheduled her for surgery. On the day of surgery, they rechecked the lump. It was gone. While skeptics decry blaming the victim for the onset of disease or other unfortunate circumstance in a person's life, proponents of the law assert that if a person can attract a negative event, she might also have the same power to eliminate it. The woman was able to restore her health through the power of her belief and positive thoughts.

You Still Need a Physician

It's been said that health is much more than the absence of disease. With the skyrocketing costs of health care, the prevailing emphasis now is on prevention of illness or disease. This means that a basic understanding of how to care for the body is important. Focused intent for good health aligned with the Law of Attraction can bring it to you. That does *not* mean you should avoid seeking treatment from a qualified physician or medical establishment if you develop an illness or other serious condition.

CRITICISM, COUNTERCRITICISM, AND CLAIMS

As the Law of Attraction ideas gained widespread attention, critics emerged from various corridors to voice concerns and divergent points of view. Those who believe in the power of the universal law found themselves defending their belief. They advised those who doubted to at least try to set aside their opposition and be open to the possibility that the law could work wonders in their lives. Their basic premise, they would tell skeptics, was that if positive thinking and a grateful attitude attract the things you want, then the flip side of that idea is that negative thinking will draw to you the things you don't want.

ATTRACT OR ALTER

Some Law of Attraction proponents have even explained that war and famine might be the culmination of a widespread pattern of negative thinking sending forth negative vibrations that attract negative events. As Rhonda Byrne, author of *The Secret*, noted, the vibrational frequency of people's thoughts match the frequency of the event thrust upon them, even though they may not have been thinking about a specific event.

Hindu and Buddhist philosophies teach detachment and the avoidance of judging experiences as either good or bad so as not to be impacted by them; however, Law of Attraction practitioners assert that it is, in fact, your thoughts that draw life experiences to you. You are not altering your relationship to (or perception of) an event. Instead, you are making it possible for it to take place through your emotions and thoughts.

DID HISTORICAL FIGURES TEACH THE LAW OF ATTRACTION?

Even as critics' voices have been rising to confront the basic tenets of the Law of Attraction and verbalize concerns about blaming victims, teachers of the law assert that many historical figures—specifically, Buddha, Hermes Trismegistus, Plato, Aristotle, Beethoven, and Isaac Newton—knew about the law and secretly taught it. They say other teachers included Winston Churchill, Thomas Edison, Carl Jung, Albert Einstein, and Andrew Carnegie. More recent teachers include mythologist Joseph Campbell and civil rights leader Martin Luther King Jr., whose most famous speech was built around the positive statement "I have a dream."

SO, WHAT DO YOU THINK?

Critics say that some Law of Attraction teachers are ridiculous to suggest that creative imagination, visualizations, affirmations, and the power of positive thinking can help a person manifest circumstances, objects, or healings. However, practitioners of the Law of Attraction point out that miraculous healings, even from seemingly incurable diseases, can and do happen. The Roman Catholic Church also acknowledges the regular occurrence of miracles. Before a person can be canonized as a saint, three miracles have to be attributed to him.

It is often difficult to assess whether an ill person has experienced a miraculous cure. Certainly, doctors can attest to the recovery, but explaining such a sudden (sometimes instantaneous) recovery in someone who has been diagnosed with a chronic affliction or terminal disease can be impossible.

Still, many people do recover through the power of their faith and unshakable belief that they will become healthy again. When they have such faith and belief in having excellent health, they set up a powerful force for attracting recovery through the Law of Attraction. For a healing to be deemed miraculous, the church undertakes a thorough investigation to rule out other possible explanations. When there is no explanation, the person's cure is deemed a miracle.

Wallace Wattles observed in his book *The Science of Getting Rich* that you shouldn't waste time daydreaming or building castles in the air, but rather stick to a vision of yourself and your purpose with all the strength of the mind you are capable of mustering. There will always be those who believe in the power of positive thinking, whether they call it the Law of Attraction or any other name. Critics will also likely continue to weigh in on whether the Law of Attraction is actually a force at work in the lives of humans. It will be up to the individual to decide to believe the critics or the advocates of the law.

CHAPTER 4

The Relationship Between the Law of Attraction and Traditional Religions

SEEKING WISDOM THROUGH MANY FACETS

Through the ages, many people have turned to religion to search for wisdom about their life's meaning and purpose. Even the ancients understood that knowledge is equated with power. During the Middle Ages, some who sought spiritual insight joined religious orders where higher learning was accessible. In the last century, seekers increasingly turned to Eastern philosophies. The 1960s and 1970s witnessed people's use of mind-expanding drugs to enter alternative states of consciousness where they believed the secrets of the universe would be revealed. Today's wisdom-seekers mine ancient traditions, science, and other sources. Let's take a closer look at how different religious beliefs intersect with the Law of Attraction.

CHRISTIANITY

The Law of Attraction works in the pursuit of spiritual desire just as it does for worldly things. Christianity emphasizes total submission of one's will to the will of God. Christian mystics have understood how the twin engines of faith and belief can merge the spiritual self into alignment and even unity with its Source. Some say that through divine grace, they entered transcendental realms and moved closer to God.

Mystics of all religions have exhibited paranormal powers, gained knowledge, and perceived truth through an inner knowing. That is not to say that all mystical experiences are pleasant. That would be too simplistic a way of defining mysticism. However, the understanding that mystics gain from time they spend in transcendental states has sometimes enabled them to manifest or create spiritual desires, often to help others. Think about how much money Mother Teresa raised in her life or about the charities founded by Vincent de Paul.

Christians believe that eternal salvation is secured by acceptance of Jesus as the Son of God and the Savior of humankind. Jesus counseled that God knows all the needs of his children. In Matthew 6:33, Jesus says to seek first the kingdom of God and his righteousness. After that, all else will be added.

CONTRADICTING CHRISTIAN BELIEFS?

Many Christians are divided on whether the Law of Attraction aligns with Christian beliefs. Those who are against the law assert that when people believe they create their lives and everything in them, they diminish or eliminate God as Creator and practice self-deification. In the Garden of Eden, the serpent promised Eve that she could have ultimate knowledge and become godlike. Eve apparently formed a strong desire to have what the serpent promised her, and so she defied God's command not to eat from the tree of the knowledge of good and evil.

Eve ate the apple and offered some of it to her mate Adam. Some people feel strongly that only God creates and that humans who desire the knowledge of universal laws and attempt to call upon the universe to help them manifest or create their lives anew put the universe before God. For some deeply devout Christians, the idea of creating a spiritual or religious life is admirable and credit should be given to the Lord. Others might say that the Lord's ways are mysterious and the Law of Attraction may be a divine mechanism to give people what they want, including drawing spiritually inspired souls closer to him.

PURSUING WEALTH OR POVERTY

People in religious orders may take a vow of poverty rather than acquire wealth and material possessions. Poverty has somehow always been equated with deeply held spiritual aspiration, whereas the pursuit of wealth often has been perceived as a selfish desire for things of the flesh instead of the spirit. The Law of Attraction, as you have already learned, is indifferent; it gives you whatever you think and feel you deserve. When you give yourself over to increase in your life, you are giving fuller expression to the abundance of the Divine Intelligence within you. However, if you seek poverty, the Law of Attraction will make it so. Proponents of the Law of Attraction say it is up to you to choose.

Christian advocates for implementation of the Law of Attraction in people's lives say, "God helps those who help themselves." They assert that people possess a powerful tool for creation, the human mind, and to not use it to better their lives and those of others wastes that precious God-given gift.

JESUS AND THE LAW OF ATTRACTION

During his years on earth, Jesus exemplified a way of living in harmony with universal laws and in keeping with his divine purpose. Today, his life and words continue to offer hope and direction for suffering souls lost in darkness or weary from their battles in life. When Law of Attraction teachers speak of the power of faith, trust, belief, vision, and declaration, they frequently cite Jesus.

THE MUSTARD SEED

Three of the New Testament Gospels—Matthew, Mark, and Luke—attribute to Jesus the comment that the kingdom of heaven is like the least of all seeds, the mustard seed that grows into the greatest of all herbs, a tree with branches to shelter the birds. Likewise, great accomplishments start with intent and small actions. When you nurture the seeds of divinity within, the Law of Attraction makes possible an unfolding of your spiritual consciousness and brings to you or guides you to the means to help yourself and others.

JESUS AND THE FIG TREE

In the New Testament Gospel of Matthew 21:21, Jesus, hungry, spied a fig tree. Noting only leaves but no fruit upon it, he said, "Let no fruit grow on thee henceforward forever." When his disciples marveled at the speed at which the tree withered, Jesus told them how they, too, could do such things. He explained that what they required was an unwavering faith and unshakable belief. They must not have any doubts that whatever they commanded to happen would occur. By believing that their desires were not only possible but probable, they could do even greater things than making a fig tree barren. They could take down a mountain and move it into the sea simply by the power of faith and belief behind their declaration of desire or intention. As quoted in the King James Version of the Bible, "Verily I say unto you, If ye have faith, and doubt not, ye shall not only do this which is done to the fig tree, but also if ye shall say unto this mountain, Be thou removed, and be thou cast into the sea; it shall be done. And all things, whatsoever ye shall ask in prayer, believing, ye shall receive." —Matthew 21:21–22

Jesus explained the means by which you can manifest your will. He said you must have faith, not doubt; clearly state your desire (for example, "Be thou removed"); ask for it; and believe that it will be done.

JESUS'S TEACHINGS

The Gospel of Luke contains a passage detailing how Jesus taught his disciples to pray. He said, "Ask, and it shall be given you; seek, and ye shall find; knock, and it shall be opened unto you. For every one that asketh receiveth; and he that seeketh findeth; and to him that knocketh it shall be opened." (Luke 11:9–10)

In the Gospel of John, Jesus offers what has come to be known as the Sermon on the Vine and the Branches. A passage within that sermon has Jesus saying, "If ye abide in me, and my words abide in you, ye shall ask what ye will, and it shall be done unto you." (John 15:7)

Living his life in tune with the purpose for which he had been sent to earth, Jesus showed through example how to love all, give much, believe all things are possible when your own power is aligned with God, and pray often with a heart of thankfulness.

In *The Secret*, Rhonda Byrne and her associates advocate seeking prosperity, abundance, inner joy, and peace, and counsel that the job of each person is to decide what she wants. Mystics have always desired to draw nearer to God and to learn how to express his love to others.

That longing for the Divine has found resonance in the lives of Christian saints from the earliest days of the church. Indeed, the manifestation of the Divine in the physical world is represented by the myriad expressions of divine love. Jesus' words in the New Testament's Gospel of John encapsulate the depth of God's love:

"For God so loved the world, that he gave his only begotten Son, that whosoever believeth in him should not perish, but have everlasting life. For God sent not his Son into the world to condemn the world; but that the world through him might be saved." —John 3:16–17

JESUS SHOWED PEOPLE HOW TO BE WHOLE

Jesus served as a spiritual beacon—"I am come a light into the world, that whosoever believeth in me should not abide in darkness" (John 12:46)—and an exemplar of how the power of God works through the human heart and mind. According to the New Testament Gospels, Jesus performed many miracles that seemingly defied the natural laws of the universe. Among other things, he fed 5,000 people with five loaves of bread and two fishes, exorcised demons, showed a mastery over nature by cursing the fig tree that then withered, raised the dead on three occasions, and healed sick people.

The Power of the Mind

Jesus emphasized having faith in God's power to bring about a particular result. He never told people that his faith had healed them, but rather that their own faith had made them whole. The power of their own minds was key. The Law of Attraction teaches that a clear vision of what you desire to manifest aligned in harmony with the Source, coupled with faith and magnetized by thought, attracts the result.

CATHOLIC MYSTICS

The mystics strove to develop a closer relationship with God by looking within. They believed that God revealed himself in ways that were not readily apparent to those who did not know what to look for or were simply unaware.

TERESA OF AVILA

Teresa of Avila was a medieval Spanish Carmelite nun whose desire for a deeper relationship with God eventually manifested as a result of her longing and effort. Teresa shocked many people, even the most devout, with her ideas about strict reform that included austere poverty, flagellation, and the wearing of sandals instead of shoes, giving rise to the term "discalced" (unshod) Carmelites. For two years, she was convinced that she was in the physical presence of Christ, although she could not see him. When she died, she left behind a rich legacy of devotional observations in her writings and her autobiography. Inspired by the Holy Spirit, Teresa yoked her desire to manifest a closer relationship with the Lord with an intention and action; that is, her adherence to a physical life of strictest poverty and renunciation. Aligned in harmony with the Law of Attraction, she got what she wanted and more. In time, she shared her spiritual gifts through her books *The Life of Saint Teresa of Avila*, *The Way of Perfection*, and *The Interior Castle*. She became the second of only three women to be named doctors of the Roman Catholic Church.

JOHN OF THE CROSS

Teresa sought help from John of the Cross to bring about reform of the Carmelite Order that involved monks. Like her, John became a mystic. He longed for silence and time for contemplation, and got both when he was incarcerated in a jail in Toledo. There, he endured both regular public lashings and isolation. During his incarceration, he wrote poetically about his suffering and love for God. His ideas and writings about the maturation of the soul and the necessity for becoming deeply attached to God would eventually result in the church also recognizing him as a doctor of the church.

HILDEGARD OF BINGEN

Yet another Christian mystic, Hildegard of Bingen, who lived several centuries before John of the Cross and Teresa of Avila, experienced visions that started in childhood and continued until her death in A.D. 1179. During medieval times, women didn't keep journals nor jot down their spiritual or ecclesiastical ideas, but Hildegard became convinced that she was being instructed by a heavenly voice telling her to record the information she gained during her ecstatic states of consciousness. Hildegard worried that she might be ridiculed by others and was reluctant to do as she was told. Eventually, however, she began dictating to her scribe what her inner visions unveiled for her. She also created musical compositions, a morality play, poetry, and works of art that revealed what she called mysteries and secrets of the Divine. Her body of work earned her high regard by the church.

When Hildegard was forty-two, a blinding light passed through her brain and conferred upon her the ability to know the meaning of religious texts. Her powerful intellect easily grasped an understanding of theology that most likely surpassed the best minds of male clerics of her time. With the blessing of Pope Eugenius (Eugene III), Hildegard produced her famous text, *Scivias* (translated alternately as *Know the Paths* or *Know the Ways of the Lord*). She likened herself to a feather lifted by the breath of God.

Hildegard perhaps exemplified the Law of Attraction's ages-old idea that "as you think, so you become." Some might say that Hildegard's prodigious works during her lifetime sprang from an inner world in which her thoughts, observations, reflections, and mystical revelation found fecund ground. Her desire to serve the Lord meant following the instructions of a heavenly voice telling her to reveal her knowledge even though her fear of condemnation literally made her ill. Nevertheless, Hildegard worked in tune with her calling and perception of truth—all in alignment with deeply held spiritual beliefs, and the Law of Attraction ensured that her inner contemplative process bore even more fruit. Her desire to serve the Lord meant expressing the knowledge she was being given.

From the interior world where she retreated to pray, meditate, and commune with the Lord, Hildegard brought forth a legacy that included more than 100 letters to religious clerics, seventy-two poems, nine books, and numerous works of art and musical compositions.

Hildegard wrote with insight and understanding about the human body and its illnesses and cures. She asserted that healing could come about through the use of things found in nature such as trees, animals, herbs, and even stones. Like a scientist, she knew how to acquire knowledge of the workings of the natural world through observation. Her intellectual fortitude, some have said, grew stronger upon a foundation of combined comprehension of religion, science, and art. Miraculous healings were attributed to her intercession.

AUGUSTINE OF HIPPO

Augustine of Hippo was endowed with a great mind and oratory skills, which he used in his service as a bishop in the early Christian church. He wrote, preached, and taught in Roman North Africa during the latter fourth century. He successfully manifested a powerful image of himself as an intellectually vibrant and a powerful orator. He made the most of his genetic endowment for intellectual inquiry and oratory and was able to attract the means to further develop them. But Augustine was willful and intensely attached to sensual pleasure, and the Law of Attraction gave him more of that too. He developed a relationship with a young girl who became his concubine for fifteen years. When Augustine deeply desired to overcome the sensual things of life that bound him and kept him from having a more personal relationship with God, he translated his desire into conviction and action. When the law began to fulfill his desire for that experience, he wrote an intensely personal account of his struggle to come to terms with his sensual nature and to know God.

In his book, *Confessions,* Augustine wrote that he came to God too late. He expressed regret that he had thrust himself upon the beautiful things that God had created instead of turning within to seek God, the Creator. According to *Confessions*, it was only after sensing a voice telling him to "take and read," was Augustine compelled to pick up a Bible where he read and obeyed a passage that instructed him to follow Christ. The Law of Attraction was at work at all times to give Augustine whatever he set his heart upon and felt driven to get—at first, stature as a hedonist and powerful orator; later, as a denunciate of hedonism and devoted follower of Christ.

HINDUISM

The Hindu faith is rooted in ancient Vedic philosophy with its inherent ideas of karmic law or the law of retribution—what you sow, you reap; also, what you send out comes back. These ideas dovetail into the Law of Attraction because what you think about most is what you draw into your life experience. Throughout an average day in your life are you thinking lovingly of the welfare of others, or falling into a pattern of criticizing others for everything that makes you unhappy and stressed out? According to the tenets of Hinduism, your thoughts are as powerful as a spoken word. Words, like your actions, are creating your karma, and when the elements are ripe for those words and actions to bear fruit (whether good or bad), they will.

When Did the Hindu Religion Begin?

Scholars have dated the origins of the Hindu religion to roughly 4000 B.C. to 2200 B.C., whereas circa 2500 B.C. has been suggested as the date for the Old Testament story about the flood and Noah's ark.

Although Hinduism is considered a polytheistic religion with as many as 33 million gods and goddesses, it teaches that at the core of all living things is Brahman, the one god who is really three gods in one—Brahma (the creator), Vishnu (the sustainer), and Shiva (the destroyer or one who brings about dissolution). Other gods and goddesses are simply manifestations of the One; this concept is summed up as unity of the Godhead.

Hindus achieve enlightenment through attunement to and alignment with the indwelling God. By becoming enlightened, individuals can attain release from the endless cycle of reincarnation, which takes place because of the karma they have created. In their spiritual work and practices, Hindus endeavor to transcend thinking in terms of duality or opposites.

The Law of Attraction principle that good thoughts and actions return good things to the doer while bad thoughts and bad actions bring more negativity and misery is an example of dualistic thinking. The idea that from one Source all things come and at their core those things are God is another example of transcendence of duality of thought. One sees unity in the many. The following is a list of beliefs that are common to many Hindu sects.

- There is one Supreme Reality (Brahman) and ultimately all souls will realize it as Truth.
- The reality of human existence is that it is nothing more than a dream in the mind of the Divine.
- There are many different paths to the realization of Brahman.
- Karma is created by a person's thoughts, words, and deeds (for good or bad) that cause the soul to reincarnate; reincarnation will continue until a soul's karma is exhausted.
- Ignorance of the innate divine nature of humans and the unity of all things creates dualistic thinking.
- Salvation (*moksha*) comes about in three ways: works, knowledge, and devotion.
- Nirvana is the complete liberation from karma, endless cycles of birth and death, and dualistic thinking.
- Liberation takes place when an individual loses her sense of self that is separate from God and instead becomes completely absorbed into the reality of the Supreme Godhead.

Spiritual well-being for most Hindus comes as a result of living a clean and decent life, observing *ahimsa* or nonviolence, serving their families, performing *dharma* (their worldly duties) and *sadhana* (spiritual practices) in the right way, and showing respect for all life forms as sacred things. Many

Hindus are vegetarians. Also, they often place high value on selfless service to others. Respect for elders is culturally ingrained in most Hindus. Mohandas Gandhi, a famous Hindu, once said that we must be the change that we seek in the world. Many Hindus seek to create a better world by first turning to the divine within to change themselves before trying to effect change in the world.

EXERCISING POWER OVER NATURE

Certain Hindu yogis, sages, siddhis, and holy persons through the ages who have committed their lives to the pursuit of truth have purportedly been able to travel through time and space at will, shrink or expand in size, abstain from food and water without damage to their physical bodies, control their heartbeat and breath, effect miracle healings, and instantly produce tangible objects through the power of thought. Some sources say the Law of Attraction finds resonance or has roots in tenets of Hinduism and shares the belief that an underlying unifying force of energy in the cosmos governs all that exists.

CHANTING, PRAYER, AND DEVOTIONAL PRACTICE

Hindu spiritual practice consists often of daily *puja* or worship at the shrine of the *ishtadeva* (one's chosen deity or form of God). To focus the mind on the spiritual realms and God, the devotee might chant a mantra or the word "Om," considered to be the cosmic sound of vibration in creation. Similarly, the core of the Law of Attraction might be summed up as thoughts having vibrations and those vibrations attract similar vibrations. To Hindus, even the name by which you are called sets up a vibration for your life.

DOING AN ANUSTHAN

To attain a specific spiritual result, a devotee, often with the guidance of a teacher or guru, will undertake a penance or fasting or an *anusthan* (specific practice often coupled with chanting, visualization, fasting, pilgrimage, or other action). This is not too different from working with the Law of Attraction with clear intent and conviction to manifest a specific result.

BUDDHISM

During almost any discussion of the Law of Attraction, the wisdom of the enlightened sage Gautama the Buddha (563 to 483 B.C.) is inevitably quoted as proof that the law has survived from ancient times until now. A favorite quote of Buddha, paraphrased here, is that each of us is the result of what we have thought. Another quote states that a person's work in life is to discover his work. Then he is to throw his whole being into doing that work. This advice, though it was offered more than 2,000 years ago, is as true today as it was then and has particular significance for understanding the psychology of the Law of Attraction, say proponents of the law.

Buddhism also says to let go of ego-centeredness. But to release the "I," you first must know the self. Practitioners must strive to understand their interconnectedness or interdependence with others and, in fact, the entire universe. These two positions seem to be opposite: me or us. The polarity must be understood—do you live your life focused purely on yourself, or do you live your life aware of your interconnectedness with others and the world?

The Four Noble Truths

The Buddha expounded four noble truths. Suffering exists; put another way, impermanence exists. Attachment to desires or craving is the origin of suffering. When attachment to desire ends, suffering ceases. Freedom from suffering is possible by following the Eightfold Path: right view, right thought, right speech, right action, right livelihood, right effort, right mindfulness, and right contemplation.

Buddhist philosophy aligns beautifully with the Law of Attraction due to its emphasis on perception, thought, speech, and action. Right thought, for example, means to harm no person or thing through negative thought, including yourself, and to avoid desire and cravings and ill will. Instead, Buddhism emphasizes cultivating thoughts of goodwill, love, joy, and gratitude. Speech should never be critical, harsh, or malevolent; instead, it should be gentle, kind, truthful, and appropriate for time and place. Having generosity of spirit and gratitude for the blessings you already have are as important in Buddhist practice as they are for deliberately working with the Law of Attraction.

What Is *Dana*?

Dana is the word used in Buddhism to mean generosity of spirit. It is perhaps best illustrated in a person's relationship with others in the form of mutual aid, trust, kindness, and commitment. Never to be obligatory, *dana* carries with it positive karma in spiritual benefits that can stretch over many lifetimes.

The idea of *dana* or generosity occupied an important place in Buddha's teachings. The act of selfless giving for the welfare of others means giving even more than is required or customary. The Buddha emphasized that one's attitude toward giving was far more important than the actual gift and, further, that the greater spiritual benefit comes to the poor person who has little but gives much than to the rich person who has much and gives something that is personally insignificant. The Buddha did not abjure the acquisition of wealth; on the contrary, he considered it a source of happiness and peace of mind if the money was gained in a morally just way.

TAOISM AND OTHER EASTERN RELIGIONS

In China, ideas about manifesting emerged in the beliefs of ancient Chinese people who were Taoist. The *Tao Te Ching* (or *Great Book of the Way and Virtue*) by Lao Tzu states that nothingness named the beginning of the universe, and haveness named all objects. The book reveals that a person makes an individual choice to have nothing and know the great wonder of the Tao, or to have objects and know abundance. Another passage says that the sage has nothing, yet lives to help others and in so helping grows richer. The sage gains even more abundance by giving to others.

Taoism contains the idea of effortless manifesting. Achieving your goal is not as important as the process that unfolds from the inception of an idea to the completion of the desired result. The miracle is that you can draw to you something you deeply desire out of the chaos, obstacles, and confusion that are all around you every day.

Taoism stresses living life from an open and loving heart space. Be attentive. Be positive. Be happy. Observe the Tao at work. Know what goal or object you desire to manifest and let that be the result you aim for, but focus on observing how the Tao operates to make it happen. You don't have to be action-oriented and try to figure out how to get that thing you want. You simply allow for the manifestation to arrive in its own perfect time. The process of its coming to you should be the focus rather than achieving the object, according to practitioners of *wu-wei,* as the art of effortlessly manifesting is known.

TAO EMPHASIS ON THE YIN

Although the Tao acknowledges the importance of male or yang qualities, it emphasizes the female or yin. Female is the polar opposite of male; yin opposes yang. Each person should, according to Lao Tzu, find a balance between yin and yang. When faced with a problem, instead of responding with a knee-jerk aggressive action (yang), remain calm and find power and peace in the stillness. Then you will know the right course to the solution. Your thoughts often propel your body into action as a response to a problematic situation. Use your thoughts and the working of the Law of Attraction to draw to yourself solutions and opportunities by remaining in a quiet mindful (yin) place. That is the way of the Tao. You are neither advancing nor retreating. You are not buffeted about by emotions. Instead, you are anchored at the center of inner strength and power.

TO POLARIZE OR NOT

Some teachers of the Law of Attraction talk about polarization, an idea that finds resonance in the *Tao Te Ching*. They assert that you can choose to live your life with a focus on none other than yourself (independent), or you can choose to live in a way that understands and accepts your interconnectedness with the whole or everything in the universe (interdependent). To choose the latter requires an understanding and acceptance that you are one part of all things that make up the whole and that all you do affects the others. To choose to polarize either way requires a measured thoughtfulness, a decision, and a commitment to live by your choice for your lifetime. Choosing one pole or the other can strengthen your intent and clarify your work with the Law of Attraction. Of course, you can also choose not to choose.

SHINTO

Shinto literally means "way of the gods" in Japanese. It can trace its roots back to antiquity in animism and nature worship. Practitioners share a deep respect for nature, believing that spirit powers live in nature and natural settings; thus, they strive to live harmoniously alongside nature and all its creatures. The notion of living in harmony with all other things, respecting and even honoring their sacredness, aligns with the Law of Attraction because such a way of living attracts more harmony, respect, and sacredness into your life.

A primary element of Shinto is a belief in *kami*, or spiritual presences. Shintoists focus on four main areas: family (because it is Shinto's linkage to tradition and the preservation of traditional beliefs and practices), sacredness of nature, bodily cleanliness (baths, mouth-rinsing, and hand-washing are done often), and celebrations to honor the kami. Shinto considers nature sacred. When Shintoists honor nature, they may create beautiful gardens and protect the places they consider to be sacred. Their respect and love for the natural world and its inhabitants, through the Law of Attraction, ensures that those special places endure and flourish. Law of Attraction practitioners could take cues from Shinto belief about the sacredness of the earth if they desire to do more for the planet, such as curbing cutting of the rainforests, aiding efforts to reduce toxic waste, working with others to find solutions to global warming, and preserving species of plants and animals.

JUDAISM AND KABBALAH

Kabbalah, the set of ancient mystical beliefs of Biblical Judaism that was once the intellectual domain of only Jewish patriarchs and prophets, is built upon precepts akin to those of the Law of Attraction. Students of Kabbalah claim that the teachings of the Kabbalah and the spiritual work they do enhances their understanding and draws them closer to God. Through the Law of Attraction, their efforts also pull to them other people who stimulate sharing of ideas and insights. Some say that the once-secret teachings may have originated with the Bible's first human—Adam. However, others assert that God gave the wisdom teachings not to Adam but rather to Moses.

Helpful Texts in the Study of Jewish Mysticism

The *Book of Formation* (*Sefer Yetzirah*) elaborates on the ecstatic experience of the Divine. The *Book of Splendor* (*Zohar*) was written in thirteenth-century Spain and expounds upon occult and metaphysical ideas. Along with the Torah and Talmud, these two texts form the basis for the study of Jewish mysticism.

Kabbalists say that the teachings contain the secrets of the universe as well as the human heart. The correct understanding of the teachings enables people to observe the chaos of the world without becoming entangled in it, as well as to maneuver through or remove the minefields of pain and suffering. The stress is upon sharpening the mind to gain clarity of thought. Teachers emphasize that all humans possess the seeds of greatness. Through Kabbalah, the potential of those seeds can manifest.

The Kabbalist idea of self-actualization (we are each accountable for ourselves, our thoughts, and our actions) resonates with Christian, Buddhist, and Hindu thinking as well as the Law of Attraction. Kabbalists believe that faith and certainty become stronger when we connect to God's light and draw down the manifestation of good into our lives.

IMPORTANCE OF MENTAL CERTITUDE

Practitioners of Kabbalah believe that they can lift themselves closer to the light of the Divine by respecting and viewing others as equals—seeing no hierarchy in humankind—and by treating others with dignity and loving service. The softening of the heart, possessing certainty of will or mind, and positive action allows greatness to manifest. This, too, seems like a reiteration of the Law of Attraction.

Rabbis from roughly the seventh to the eighteenth centuries developed the mystical method of Kabbalah to interpret and explain Scripture. Two main ideas of Kabbalah state that all of creation emanates from God, and that the soul is eternal. Another important concept is that humankind (the microcosm) mirrors the Divine (the macrocosm). Finally, an understanding and use of Kabbalah can enable us to transcend our karma.

Kabbalah 101

The word Kabbalah means to "to receive, to accept." Many translators attribute the meaning "tradition" to the term. Some sources say the Kabbalah, which offers an esoteric interpretation of the Scriptures, was given with the Torah, but whereas the Torah was meant for the masses, the Kabbalah was intended for the holiest ones who then orally passed on its secrets to Jewish mystics.

OPENING UP TO THE SACRED

When you desire to gain deep spiritual insights, study of sacred books draws you deeper into the world of ideas of spiritual thinkers and holy people. These are people who may have spent their lives in an intellectual and heartfelt pursuit of the Divine. Aligning your mind with those whose ideas appeal to you draws in more sources for similar thought because you are open to seeing such ideas everywhere. Your conversations with others may drift to a particular spiritual concept that confuses you, and you may find clarity. You may pick up a book that elucidates a concept or philosophy perfectly. The Law of Attraction is at work at all times to help you find myriad sources to fulfill your desire for more knowledge, insights, and understanding when you feel passionate about a topic.

Since ancient times, rabbis and students of Kabbalah have turned to the symbolism of numbers, images, colors, and words to decipher and explain the ecstatic experience of God. One important and necessary image for the study of Kabbalah is the Tree of Life with its ten orbs and twenty-two paths.

ECSTATIC KABBALAH

There are different paths for the study of Kabbalah. The path known as Ecstatic Kabbalah emphasizes recitation of divine names or combinations of the pure forms of the letters of the Hebrew alphabet. The iteration or chanting of divine names, fueled by a noble desire to attain greater understanding and insights into the Divine, inspires loftier spiritual thoughts and thus sets up a corresponding attraction via the universal Law of Attraction to draw to the Kabbalist an expansion of consciousness, perhaps even a state of ecstasy.

NEW AGE

New Age philosophy, according to some people, is nothing less than a religion. Others say it lacks the attributes of other established world religions, most of which have some type of dogma or creed, traditions, and specific teachings that bind believers together. New Age thinking, in comparison, stresses an individualistic approach to spirituality that includes an eclectic melding of religious, scientific, self-help, psychological, and ecological ideas, among others. Although experts on the Law of Attraction say the principle of the law is ancient, the popular use of that universal law fits well within New Age thought and its emphasis on the connection between the body, mind, and spirit.

The Human Potential Movement, popular in the 1960s and 1970s, was a New Age movement that emphasized the notion that humans possessed infinite potential and were limited only by negative thoughts or traditional beliefs. The main goal in the Human Potential Movement was to replace a negative mindset with positive thinking. Today, that goal encapsulates the idea of how to best work with the Law of Attraction to be all that you can be and to have abundance.

One of the most controversial and popular programs to emerge out of the New Age Human Potential Movement was est (Erhard Seminars Training). Founder Werner Erhard advocated est as a way for people to undergo personal transformation and attain empowerment. People were taught to take responsibility for their lives and what they were manifesting, good and bad. Erhard reportedly gave credit to his study of Zen Buddhism to create the space in which the concept of est was to emerge.

MAGICK

Pagan magick is a religious practice to many. A report by the *Chicago Tribune* stated that Neo-Paganism is one of the fastest growing religions in the United States today. The Wicca religion is a form of pagan witchcraft that espouses belief in a Goddess and God, dual but complementary polarities, and is based in nature. It is difficult to estimate the number of Neo-Pagans because many are solitary practitioners. Some, however, do assemble together to practice their rites. Their spells often utilize special magickal tools to manifest the desires of an individual or group.

Magick has its origins in the ancient world, but modern experts on the Law of Attraction say the law itself is nothing less than magick. Perhaps you could find the pot of gold at the rainbow's end or be like King Midas of

Greek mythology and turn everything you touch into gold by working with the law. However, skeptics might ask why the medieval alchemists, who were using all the knowledge about magick available to them, were unable to produce gold out of base metals. Was it really that their belief was not strong enough? Did they not have faith? Did they not magnetize their thoughts enough?

Such questions seldom faze proponents of the Law of Attraction. If you want gold, some proponents of the law suggest writing a blank check for a certain amount of money and signing it The Universe, Keeper of the Universe's Storehouse, or God(dess) of Abundance, for example, and to expect it to manifest. Working along with the Law of Attraction for wealth, you might try to express enthusiastic optimism while thinking positive thoughts about the money coming and have faith that financial prosperity is going to manifest in your life by the power of your thought, even if you can do nothing else.

Theurgy 101

Theurgy was a system of magic based on the belief that practitioners would be aided by the gods with whom they communicated. Platonists (followers of the Greek philosopher Plato), for example, believed that physical objects were merely representations of unchanging ideas. They thought it possible to communicate with the gods and to receive divine help in manifesting.

ORIGINS OF MAGICK

If you were to attempt to trace the lineage of magicians back in time, you would most likely discover stories about the Magi, the Assyrian-Babylonian learned men and high priests of what was once a Mesopotamian tribe. In ancient times, magick and religion were co-mingled. Zarathustra, who lived circa 600 B.C. in what is now known as Iran, for example, is considered the father of magick in ancient history. The Greeks pronounced his name Zoroaster, and the religion by which he was associated as Zoroastrianism.

Egyptian magic utilized the power of names. To name something was to have the ability to claim its power or exercise some authority over it. They held dreams to be communication from the gods, believed in dream incubation, and even understood how to place an order for a dream. Mummification involved both a religious practice and rituals of magic. Modern practitioners of the law say you can use the Law of Attraction's power to draw to you something that you desire by naming it, declaring and writing its name often, affirming your desire to have it, and expressing gratitude that you know it is on its way to you in this moment.

The Connection Between Shamanism and the Egyptians

Shamanism possibly had primitive beginnings among the ancient Egyptians, who believed in nature magic and fiercely protected their wisdom traditions relating to such. In Iraq and Iran, archeologists found earthenware vessels (Babylonian demon bowls) featuring nature motifs that may have been used to cast spells, or trap or protect against demons in nature.

The polytheistic Egyptian magicians participated in spellcasting, and loved talismans and sacred objects. Because their priests were the keepers of ancient wisdom and the only ones who could be magicians, they were reluctant to share such knowledge with others. Perhaps they understood the Law of Attraction, because under the Pharaohs, Egypt experienced increase—at least for a while.

CELTS

The ancient Celts of Wales, Ireland, Scotland, and parts of Western Europe perceived magic everywhere and in everything. Celts worshiped many deities, among them the earth mother and the horned god. They shared a deep reverence for the earth, believed in faeries and nature spirits we would call elves and gnomes, and honored the four elements of nature (air, earth, fire, and water). The Celts willfully suspended disbelief and saw magic manifested in their daily lives. Scholar, poet, and philosopher John

O'Donohue noted in his book *Anam Cara: A Book of Celtic Wisdom* that the Celtic people in the west of Ireland had legends and stories in which there were bridges between the visible and invisible worlds. For example, the locals might not cut down a bush in a field for generations because they knew the faeries had long ago built a fort in that place. Their prevailing thoughts came about through a strong and powerful tradition, and undoubtedly brought, by means of the Law of Attraction, incidences and manifestations that further enhanced and deepened their magical beliefs.

MODERN MAGICK

Long before the Gaia hypothesis and the modern philosophy of integrative medicine, with its emphasis on the mind/body connection, Paracelsus, a sixteenth-century alchemist, astrologer, and occultist, proposed a radical idea for his time. He asserted that the natural world was a living organism that expressed the One Life. Further, he postulated that humankind and the universe were one in essence, and that a magnetic attraction existed between each part of the human and the corresponding part in nature. Health depended upon a harmony between man and nature, a concept known as the Doctrine of Signatures. Paracelsus did not think of himself as a magician, although others did.

Just as medieval alchemy blurred the lines between magic, religion, and science, the boundaries between modern magick and religion also are blurred. A student of modern magick may learn about not only rituals, gems, spells, symbols, Hebrew letters, Kabbalah, occultism, and alchemy, but must also understand the power of declarations, incantations, and intention.

Jung and Magick

Carl Gustav Jung, the Swiss psychiatrist, writer, and student of Sigmund Freud, studied magick and alchemy, presumably for insights into human psychology. Likewise, the prolific English writer Aleister Crowley, a contemporary of Jung, studied astrology, the occult, and sex magick, and was a member of a number of secret societies.

Modern magick, like the magic of the ancients, represents a spiritual path for some seeking wisdom and higher truths. Getting specific results involves utilizing the power of one's thoughts, words, and deeds, something it shares with the Law of Attraction.

PART 2

The Law of Attraction Exercises

In this section, you'll find more than 50 exercises, techniques, and ideas that you can use to help yourself stay focused on the Law of Attraction every day. You'll be focused on implementing the law using these six simple steps:

1. **Accept that you deserve what you desire:** What you fervently desire is sure to manifest when you give yourself permission to have it, think about it often and with feeling, consider ways to acquire it, and set in motion the acquisition of it through your intent.

2. **Form your intention:** When you desire something deeply and form an intention to acquire it, you will begin to turn over in your mind ways that you might have the object of your desire. Intent to have something usually triggers strong emotional

feelings such as excitement and happiness. You feel motivated to work for it. You imagine yourself in the state you desire.

3. **Believe that you will attain your desire:** When desire is coupled with intent and motivation, you begin to believe that you can attain the object you desire. You allow yourself to wrap your mind around the happiness and pride you would feel when you would finally attain what you want.

4. **Have a positive attitude:** Belief that you can have your desire must be sustained because there surely will be a period between dreaming of having it and the physical manifestation of it in your life. You must believe that your desire is already en route to you, as if it was already decided and it was simply a matter of waiting until it showed up. You never question how or when; you just keep your faith.

5. **Show gratitude:** Intensify your efforts of deliberately working with the Law of Attraction by feeling and expressing your thankfulness at what you already have. Feel gratitude for the power that is working to bring you the object you fervently desire. Each day as you go to work, spend the time thanking God or the universe for your many blessings.

6. **Receive:** Be ready to receive. Sometimes that means making space in your life, your home, your business, or your jewelry box for the object of your desire. Always be prepared for your desire to come to you.

1

Assess Your Life

Proponents of the Law of Attraction assert that every person can create a life of wealth, abundance, and happiness that otherwise might seem improbable or impossible and defies logic and reason. If a review of your life and the goals you had established makes you feel happy, it's likely you accomplished those things. On the other hand, if you feel sad or disappointed, you likely did not accomplish them. Here's a little quiz that might get you motivated to leverage your life with the Law of Attraction.

1. What do you like about your life?
2. What drives your passion?
3. What gets you energized and sets your head spinning with new ideas?
4. What personal growth do you desire for your life?
5. Where do you want to be in your career/job this time next year? In five years?
6. What do you desire your life to be like?
7. What do you desire to add to your life that is currently not in it?
8. What one new thing would you like to manifest right now?

Follow your passion, even if you have little money and no formal training or degrees to qualify you. You'll know you are on the fast track to success when you feel good doing that which fuels your passion. The Law of Attraction states that like attracts like. Feelings magnetize your desires, and magnetized desires attract more of the same and propel you forward in your passionate endeavors to success.

2

Brainstorm What You Really Want

How do you decide what you want to attract in your life? Close your eyes and think of something that you either want or need that would make you incredibly happy. Set aside your doubt and pretend for a moment that anything you want is possible. If doubt floods your mind, start small and continue taking baby steps in your manifesting efforts until you have proven to yourself how easy it is.

Is what you want to manifest an object, such as a new lipstick, a paella pan, or a fountain for your garden? Is it situation you'd like to bring about, such as improving your health, securing a promotion, or mastering a tennis serve? Is it something you want to do for the world, such as write a book, establish a business, or create a masterful work of art? It's best to develop a crystal-clear idea of the object of your desire and stick with it.

Think of how much you enjoy browsing through the pictures in your favorite catalogs, spending a day at the outlet stores, or whiling away an hour or two at a Costco or Sam's Club warehouse. Now consider all the offerings of every store, merchant, or collective. Remember, you are shopping in the warehouse of the universe. The promise of the law is that if you can imagine and desire something clearly enough, using high levels of creative energy, you can swiftly attract it.

3

Write a Mission Statement for Your Life

Companies often create mission statements to tell the public and their employees exactly what their company stands for. You can do the same for your own life! To get started, read the following list, adding principles or values that are important to you and crossing out those that are not important. Narrow the list to the eight core principles that you believe are critical to your life. Eliminate five of the eight. The remaining three are your most important core principles.

- Self-acceptance
- Career
- Fame
- Family
- Friendship
- Happiness
- Health
- Honesty
- Inclusion of others
- Integrity

- Joy
- Justice
- Love
- Peace
- Power
- Recognition
- Spirituality
- Status
- Wealth
- Wisdom

To create a mission statement, write a paragraph for each of these three values about what they mean to you when you experience success in them. Finally, merge the three paragraphs together to create a powerful mission statement for your life. This statement can help guide your intentions and strengthen your connection to the Law of Attraction.

4

Create Space in Your Life for Your Intentions

Release what isn't working in your life and open your heart and mind to allow in new energy, relationships, and surprises that the universe may be ready to give you. Sometimes when the things you desire don't readily appear, you have to make space for them. For example, if a relationship has soured and counseling or other avenues for repairing it have not helped, it may be time to move on. If your life seems stalled because your career has hit an impasse, your job doesn't inspire you, or everywhere you look things are broken, outdated, or not used, bless and release them.

To do this, reprogram your thoughts. Your outer life is a manifestation of your inner thoughts and feelings. When you release old patterns of negative thinking and replace them with powerful positive thoughts and expectations that make you feel hopeful and happy, you set into motion vibrations that can then attract an abundance of good things to you. Do you desire love with a partner who is trustworthy, capable, and emotionally healthy? Examine your thoughts to see why this individual is not already in your life. Maybe the pain and drama associated with a previous relationship caused you to fear a future one. But if you can't imagine the possibility of a wonderful new love, how will it ever come to you?

5

Visualize Your Intention

Law of Attraction experts advocate using visualization when you are deliberately working with the law because your body responds to the feelings created by positive mental images and thoughts. Choose one of the following topics and focus on, fantasize, and visualize as though you had already achieved phenomenal success in that area.

As you visualize (no negative feelings or thoughts allowed), focus on how you feel as you place yourself in your chosen scenario. Allow any/all details to unfold in your mind's eye. Write down any insights or ideas for goals, timelines, and specific action steps for quicker attainment of your desire.

1. Financial prosperity/wealth
2. Romantic love or partner
3. Birth of a child or pet project
4. Robust health
5. Peaceful life or exciting life of travel and new experiences
6. Career advancement or establishing/running your own business
7. Meaningful and passionate work/journey in life
8. Spiritual advancement

Feel free to add your own special desire to the list. Reinforce your visualization work by doing one or more of the following:

- Write a desire/intention declaration or vision statement.
- Create a manifestation poster (using images, words, symbols, and statements clipped from magazines and glued to the poster) for what you want to create or manifest.
- Record in your journal all the positive feelings you experience whenever you visualize your desire actualized in your life.

6

Complete This Intention-Setting Worksheet

This exercise is designed to help you clarify your desire to manifest an object. You know what you want, but if you were asked to describe that item in detail, could you do it? The universe will bring you exactly what you ask for, so it is important that you be specific. When you see something you want, you will perhaps remember only the general shape, maybe the color, and perhaps a detail or two. Use this exercise to establish a clear statement of your intention for manifesting a particular object with as many details as possible.

1. Name the category of the material thing you most desire to manifest (for example: car, house, boat, jewelry, furniture, art, musical instrument, dishware, clothing, or electronic item).

2. Name the specific item make or style (for example, a car might be a Mercedes S500; a musical instrument might be a Gibson folk guitar or a Stradivarius violin; an electronic item might be a Toshiba Satellite Pro laptop or seventy-five-inch plasma screen television).

3. What is its color?

4. What size and shape does it have? If you don't know, find a picture of the object you desire on the Internet or in a magazine and cut it out. Knowing what it looks like will be important for your visualization exercises.

5. What does it taste like? Of course, this may not be relevant to the object you desire to manifest, but if it happens to be a 100-year-old bottle of Scotch, being able to imagine the taste will be important.

6. Does it have a scent? If so, write down your thoughts about what it smells like (new clothes or wooden instruments may have subtle scents, for example, while a piece of china probably will not have a scent).

7. What does it sound like? Sound may not have relevance for some objects but for cars, musical instruments, computers, or electronic equipment, the sound it makes is an important detail.

8. Mentally run your fingers over the object of your desire. How does it feel? What is its texture?

7

Re-Order Your To-Do List to Reduce Stress

Stress can be a good thing. It triggers alertness when we need it—for example, when we give a speech or perform for others. Stress also prepares us to react instantly to danger. During a healthy stress response, norepinephrine, an excitatory neurotransmitter that is necessary to create new memories, is released.

Everyone feels stress from time to time, but unrelenting stress, the kind you might experience in a high-pressure job, can wreak havoc on your health—and your ability to tap into the Law of Attraction. According to several sources, 75 to 90 percent of all visits to the doctor may be attributed to stress-related ailments and cost the U.S. economy in excess of $300 billion annually.

Doctors refer to stress without relief as distress. Patients suffering distress have a chronic oversecretion of stress hormones that exerts an adverse cumulative effect on brain function and memory. When the brain is constantly flooded with those powerful hormones designed only for short-term release during emergency situations, the result can be damage and death to brain cells. Some patients suffering a lifetime of chronic stress experience impairment of long-term memory. Distress can trigger emotional disorders and contribute to a plethora of bodily ailments, including the following:

- Anxiety
- Arthritis
- Asthma
- Brain function and memory loss
- Depression

- Diabetes
- Headaches
- Heart problems
- High blood pressure
- Insomnia and sleep problems
- Skin problems

It is not necessary to completely eliminate stress, but rather to effectively manage it in order to attract optimum health in alignment with the Law of Attraction. Do you feel totally stressed out and exhausted at the end of your day? Had you overscheduled yourself? One way to assess whether or not you're trying to do too much is to work with a list of daily tasks. Prioritize your list into things that only you can do and work you can delegate to others. Of the things only you can do, reorder the list so that the tasks you dread the most (and likely most stressful) are spaced out with other tasks that you love to do. The point is to create balance between work you dread and work you love. Evaluate how you feel after a day of using the new list to see if you managed to reduce your high levels of anxiety and stress.

8

Set Your Intention While in a "Neutral" Mood

An effective reinforcement tool for working with the Law of Attraction is an understanding of how your mood affects your ability to attract the results you desire. It may be more difficult than you think to understand how external and internal thoughts can trigger feelings that translate to good or bad moods. Yet such knowledge can be a powerful aid in your manifestation efforts. You'll know what your mood triggers are, and recognizing them can help you to quickly redirect a negative mood or reinforce a positive one.

Mood is the best indicator of your emotion. The happiness and passion you feel when you do work you love can quickly change into hurt when someone criticizes you. You may even become angry and desire to lash out at that person. In a short span of time, you've just experienced three emotions.

You must learn to identify the state of mind that is best suited for making decisions. Many feelings and emotions can impede your ability to make good decisions, and learning to control them can be very helpful in working with the Law of Attraction.

Basic Types of Emotions

1. Love
2. Surprise
3. Happiness
4. Fear
5. Sadness
6. Anger

You don't want to be asked to make a decision when you are in a bad mood. Why? If you are in such a mood and are asked to decide something, you are likely to revisit negative memories and anticipate negative consequences to your decision. However, if you are in a good mood when you are asked to make a decision, you may anticipate a positive outcome to your answer based on your good feelings. Make important decisions—and set your intentions—when you are in a neutral mood. Then neither positive nor negative emotions can unduly wield influence over reasoning and logic in your decision-making process.

9

Make Your Intention Crystal Clear

Clarity of intention brings faster and stronger results. Don't engage in wishful thinking and then forget about what you wanted. When your thoughts, emotion, and intention are aligned 100 percent on achieving the optimal outcome, you will achieve greater success. Conversely, when you slide into a place of lower expectation and dilute the intention to have the best, then you may fail to achieve your desired goal.

Be clear about your intention to have exactly what you want. How?

- Hold in your mind the image of your desired object. See the colors, the detailing, the size, the weight, the opacity or clarity.
- Determine the time frame within which you want it in your life.
- Do whatever you can to mentally see it in its totality by envisioning yourself using it or enjoying it.
- Think of all the ways it might come to be in your possession.

Know that it is already in the universe and on its way.

10

Actually Write Down Your Intention

Now that you have employed your senses of sight, taste, touch, smell, and hearing in order to better imagine the object you intend to manifest, write a simple declaration of your intention. Here an example to get you started.

I am elated to know that the Law of Attraction is in the process

of bringing into my life the _____

_____

that I deeply desire. I can see it clearly in my mind now (mentally

imagine it) and am grateful (feel the gratitude) that it already exists

in the realm of pure potentiality. I deserve this, am ready to receive

it, and know that it is on its way to me, and at the right moment it

will manifest in my life.

_____

Signature

11

Express Desire in the Right Language

When you are asked about your desire, if you say, "I want to stop dating losers," you are putting yourself in position to continue attracting them. "Loser" is an emotionally potent word for people. It's so negative that it is the strongest word in that sentence. Find other words and phrasing to express your desire for a healthy relationship with an emotionally mature individual who is right for you. Think carefully about how you are asking for things.

Instead of saying, "I need to get out of this lousy job," try saying instead, "I am manifesting meaningful work in my field of _____ that pays three times my current salary of _____, and I'll be working in that position by _____."

According to teachers of the Law of Attraction, when you form a strong intentional desire, you shake up the status quo. Even if you aren't doing things to fulfill your desire, you have initiated a shift in your thinking. That, in turn, sets up a new energy that opens the way for new objects, opportunities, and individuals to show up in your life.

12

Have a Positive Attitude, No Matter What

Do you believe that most humans are innately good? Do you think each person has an awesome power to have the life he chooses? Do you seek the lesson in every good and bad experience that comes into your life? When you experience a moment of high drama, do you . . .

- Remember to take some deep breaths?
- Try to depersonalize the situation?
- See what there is to learn from the way the situation is unfolding?

These are all examples of having a positive attitude.

Having a good attitude when life is beating up on you can be challenging. When your finances are going south, when your wife has dumped you for her personal trainer, when your car has just been keyed, it's difficult to see any good. But that is exactly the time to cultivate a positive attitude. When the darkness swirls around you, look for the light.

When you have a great attitude, are focused on and energetically pursuing your goal, and always have a bright smile and a kind word for others, you will attract other like-minded people.

Make yourself into a beacon of bright light and optimism. Express positive feelings and a grateful attitude for what's good in your life, and let those feelings extend outward into the lives of all those you know and love. Don't give much energy to the things that aren't working for you. Try to be an observer in the drama and, as you seek whatever goodness you can find, watch how the energy begins to shift. At times, it can be positively palpable.

13

Energize Your Intention with Actions

One way to energize intentional thought is by mapping out an action or to-do list. Think about some of the things you might do to set up a powerful magnetic attraction, drawing to you the object of your desire. Clean the garage, for example, to make possible a space to park that new sports car you want. Throw a party and invite single people; ask everyone to bring a friend. Who knows—that new romantic partner you desire might just show up.

Thoughts become more powerful when they are magnetized by your emotion. Intent becomes energized through repetitive thinking of the same thoughts and by clarity of focus. It's also important to know your reasons for wanting something. It will usually have to do, in part, with how it makes you feel. Dare to dream larger than life itself.

By allowing your thoughts to frequently visit your desire and by opening your heart to feel the positive emotions of joy and happiness, you are supporting your intention and strengthening the pull of the Law of Attraction. You are drawing toward yourself that which is already in infinite potentiality. But it bears repeating here that you must be vigilant about your thoughts. Negative situations, people, and objects drift into your life when you worry, are afraid, and feel stressed. But when you are happy, are grateful, and feel empowered, more good things manifest.

14

Tune Into Higher Vibrations to Connect with the Universe

Hindu spiritual practice consists often of daily *puja*, or worship at the shrine of the *ishtadeva* (one's chosen deity or form of God). To focus the mind on the spiritual realms and God, the devotee might chant a mantra or the word "Om," considered to be the cosmic sound of vibration in creation. Similarly, the core of the Law of Attraction might be summed up as thoughts having vibrations and those vibrations attract similar vibrations. To Hindus, even the name by which you are called sets up a vibration for your life.

Here's a little technique to try in order to consciously raise your vibration. It's easy and just takes a few minutes. Try recording this in a soft voice with long pauses between the steps. Play it back once you are sitting comfortably with your eyes closed.

1. Sit comfortably with your eyes closed.
2. Inhale a cleansing breath. Exhale stress and negativity. Do this three times.
3. Turn your closed eyes gently upward to the point between your eyebrows and focus there. Imagine powerful rays of light pouring into your head, filling you with warm, holy light as you feel yourself slightly spinning or rising.
4. Listen for a little buzz, the cosmic vibration of atoms throughout creation, and focus on that.
5. Relax and sink even deeper, especially in the spaces between your breaths. Bask in the peace. Feel love radiating out of your heart's energy center to everyone who needs love.
6. Mentally affirm that you are going to count slowly to five and that when you reach five, your energy vibration will automatically rise. As you count, feel the rays flowing in. They are warmer, but not beyond your comfort level. Hear the buzzing sound more loudly. Feel yourself floating higher. You have just raised your vibration. Do you feel the difference?

15

Believe in Your Self-Worth

Mental health professionals say that it is unhealthy to "stuff" your emotions. Instead, you are encouraged to express feelings in positive ways in order to process them. Getting to the root of anger, for example, is an important precursor to working with the Law of Attraction, because once you know what triggers it you can deal with the cause, then forgive and release. Working on your self-esteem proves easier once old issues have been resolved. It's important that you feel worthy and deserving of the good things in life, and that you develop a success consciousness.

Your brain is a repository of memory and feeling. It takes a lot of energy to hold resentment, shame, hatred, and ideas of retribution inside. Seek professional help before probing emotionally potent psychological wounds because the process can sometimes trigger mental health issues. Your brain is the most powerful manifestation tool you have. It needs care and attention for it to perform its role in working with the Law of Attraction.

16

Embrace Expectation and Anticipation

Expecting to receive what you desire is vital to getting it. A heightened sense of expectation intensifies the vibration of your thought whenever you dare to expect that the thing, person, or circumstance you desire is yours to be had. Allowing yourself to feel a sense of expectation reinforces the attraction or pull of it to you.

Expectation evolves into a sense of anticipation when you believe so strongly that what you desire is on its way to you that you accept it without doubt. Pleasure levels rise within you. You are excited, eager, and happy. Consider the following example of simple pleasure: a toddler, separated from his loving parents during their long workday, looks up to see one of them entering the room. The child's sudden recognition causes him to feel happiness.

When your anticipatory feelings of expectation coincide with the actual event finally occurring, a heightened state of pleasure sets in. Think of a time when something wonderful happened to you. When you recall that experience, how do you feel? Happy again? Now think about something you deeply desire that you know at some point is going to show up in your life—for example, getting a promotion with a huge pay increase, finding the love of your life, conceiving a child, receiving a scholarship, or buying your dream house. The happiness grows in intensity, doesn't it?

When working with the Law of Attraction, whether you simply imagine positive feelings or really feel them doesn't matter. But if you spend five minutes imagining the elation you'll feel at getting your heart's desire and then fifty-five minutes of every hour doubting that the law is really going to work, you are sabotaging your efforts. Further, you are blocking the manifesting of what you want.

17

Strengthen Your Intention by Attracting the Right Kind of Energy

If you want something badly enough, what do you do? You tell everyone you meet. Let's say it's a baby grand piano. You talk about it, think about it, look at pictures of it, visit piano stores, run your fingers up and down the keyboards, dream of what it feels like to finally have one of your own, and go to sleep with the piano on your mind. You listen to piano music, read the biographies of great pianists, and dream of playing your own baby grand at parties or recitals. You feel shivers of delight at the mere thought of owning such a beautiful piano. You may even jump up and down and exclaim, "My piano is here!" That's creating heat around your desire. You are going to pull that piano into your life.

Affirming the belief that what you desire is coming to you is the best way to deflect doubt when it creeps in. Trust that what you want is on its way, and give thanks for that. Sidestep the details of how and when it's coming. Let the Source handle those. You focus on reinforcing desire and intention through all means available.

18

Implement the Techniques of Manifestation

You can reinforce and intensify your efforts through an understanding of the four techniques of manifestation.

1. **Focus on having abundance rather than lack in your life.** Establish a routine of setting aside certain times throughout the day to consider the abundance that already exists in your life. Discover what makes you feel alive and passionate. Pursue that and the universe will support you. Count your blessings and feel grateful, but also expect that your desires await you if you summon them through emotionally charged positive thinking.

2. **Establish the intention to manifest your desire with goals and then magnetize your intention with confidence and certitude of achieving positive results.** Allow your mind to wrap around your desire and all the various ways you can help the Law of Attraction bring that person, circumstance, or thing into your life. It doesn't hurt to develop specific goals and ideas about opportunities to watch for in order to attain your desire, but don't get too bogged down with how your desire can manifest. Don't forget to consider why you want to manifest your desire, what you will do with it, and how it will make you feel. Also consider whether or not your desire is going to hurt someone else; for example, coveting your best friend's car or boyfriend is a not a healthy choice and should never be the object of your desire.

3. **Cultivate conviction and make ready to receive.** Know with your heart, mind, and soul that the object of your desire is en route to you at this very moment. This does not suggest a total passivity on your part. (Refer to Technique 2.) Allow the object to come into your life. Because you claim the destiny of the object of your desire, practice seeing yourself having it. Let yourself experience joy and the satisfaction of finally having your desire wash over you again and again.

4. **Develop an attitude of gratitude and express appreciation often**—
not only to others (even pets) for their gifts of love and friendship,
but also to the Source or the Creator. Allow yourself to feel as if you
have forever been and always will be in the protective and capable
hands of the Divine. Let go of all worry and feel serene, peaceful,
happy, and grateful.

19

Balance Your Giving and Receiving

How good a receiver are you? Many people are wonderful at giving, but not so adept at receiving. You need to be a good receiver to work with the Law of Attraction to create what you want in life. Think about the messages you might have heard growing up about giving and receiving. "It's better to give than receive" is an often-quoted phrase from the Bible. The phrase was specific to tithing, to giving what was needed to those institutions that provided spiritual support and sustenance. As with all things, giving and receiving is an exchange of energies. In fact, giving and receiving are the same energy.

Try this exercise:

1. Draw a straight line on a piece of paper. Place an arrow pointing away from the line at either end. At the right end, write the word *giving*, and at the left end, write the word *receiving*.
2. Assume that the midpoint of the line would be the point of true reciprocity, where giving and receiving come into balance. Think about where you are on that line. Are you usually giving, or is your giving-and-receiving scale balanced?

You can also think of giving and receiving as a circle. As you move along the rim of the circle you are giving out energy, yet energy from elsewhere is moving around the circle and being offered to you. Do you have your back to the energy being offered? Or are you receptive to what is coming your way? Are you aware of the cycle of giving and receiving?

Being open to receiving means you are learning to be open to the opportunities the universe has been waiting to give you. Once you initiate your co-creative energy through your intention and desire, the Law of Attraction begins to work. Opportunities to move you along the path of manifestation start to come your way in the form of people, new job prospects, unexpected gifts, and even new financial abundance.

Look at your patterns of giving. Are you giving your time, energy, resources, or material possessions for reasons other than a spontaneous impulse of generosity of spirit? If so, you might be tied into self-limiting beliefs about the need to please and conform. When you understand patterns of giving you can truly receive the wonderful opportunities the universe has for you. When you over-give, you under-receive. If you want to strengthen your capacity for receiving, try asking for help. Admit a mistake. Let others know you are emotionally vulnerable and need their support.

20

Learn Other Laws Related to the Law of Attraction

It's a good idea to have an understanding of other metaphysical laws that may directly affect the outcome of your spiritual work with the Law of Attraction. As you go through the steps of working with the Law of Attraction, consider how these others laws may be working in your own life.

Universal Laws Affecting Manifestation

1. **The Law of Intention:** To work with this law, know why you are doing what you are doing, as well as how your actions attract good and bad to you.

2. **The Law of Karma:** Be aware that your every thought, word, and deed triggers a reaction in the universe. Think of it as "you reap what you sow" or "what you send out returns to you." In Buddhism, whether good or bad happens, it is not God or the Creator causing those things, but karma. Every thought, word, and act has a consequence, according to Buddhists. A person must let go of attachment, be still and observant, and discover what is real and what is not.

3. **The Law of Continuity:** Remember that energy and matter do not die, but can be transformed.

4. **The Law of Synchronicity:** Take notice of how, once you've decided to manifest something, references to it start showing up in your life frequently in a multitude of ways.

21

Take a Break from Negative Messages

Reduce the amount of negativity you will tolerate. Americans are bombarded every day by advertising messages that emphasize dissatisfaction and lack in your life. Some sources say that the average person receives more than 1,000 negative messages each day. Ask yourself how you eliminate negative messages in order to raise your level of life satisfaction.

Psychologist Martin Seligman, PhD., noted for his contributions to the idea of learned helplessness and depression, decided to study the factors that enable people to have positive emotional health. His research led to an area of psychology known as positive psychology or optimal human functioning. People are more likely to experience vibrant physical health and feel less stress when they have a high level of life satisfaction.

In his research on optimism, Seligman discovered five primary factors out of twenty-four associated with high levels of life satisfaction. The five were optimism, curiosity, the ability to give and receive love, a zest for life, and gratitude. Seligman asserted that of those five factors, gratitude was the most important one associated with happiness. Visit *www.authentichappiness.sas .upenn.edu/* for more information.

A cautionary word about bad habits might be useful here, too. Bad habits such as overindulgence in food or drink sabotage your efforts to lose weight and manifest a sleeker, healthier self. Chronic tardiness decreases your chances for manifesting success at school or work. Lack of focus scatters your energies and undermines your efforts to produce the results you desire in every area of your life. Avoidance issues impede your ability to solve problems and to clear the way for the manifestation of your dreams. Overlay your bad habits with good ones. Make a commitment to repeat the good habit until it takes hold, displacing and eventually replacing the bad one.

22

Repeat Positive Affirmations

The Law of Attraction responds to your feeling. When you say an affirmation that resonates with you, your affirmation becomes positive. But when you make a desire declaration or say an affirmation that is not true for you, your feeling is conflicted because you have doubts that it can really be true. Doubt cancels out your desire and blocks manifestation.

Your choice of words or use of language differs depending on whether you are in a negative or a positive mood. The brain cannot hold both negative and positive emotions at the same time, say Law of Attraction teachers. You will experience either positive or negative polarity, and it will be reflected in your inner dialogue word choices.

When you are in a bad mood and your mental thought vibration is negative, you use words like *no, not, can't, won't, don't,* and *impossible.* But when you feel upbeat and happy, you use positive expressions like *yes, can, will, do,* and *possible.* When you say *can't, won't, don't,* and *no,* you are focusing your attention on what you do not want; the mind sifts the negative contractions out of the statement and zeroes in on what remains. For example, the statement, "I don't want any more bills," brings you more bills.

Try substituting a positively phrased question, like "What is my deepest desire?" Then express what you want using positive language and avoiding those negative words. For example, instead of saying, "I can't get the job of my dreams; I'm not good enough," say instead, "I am excited to be in the process of getting the job of my dreams because I am skilled at what I do and am passionate about doing it." Give focused attention and energy to your positive affirmation statements.

Proper phrasing makes a desire more attainable. If you were an aspiring writer, your affirmation might go something like, "I am in the process of becoming a successful writer because I am creating more compelling and believable scenes for my play every day." This imprints upon the conscious and subconscious mind that the individual is already working toward the result.

If you have a pattern of attracting unhealthy relationships but you make a desire declaration that you have healthy and loving relationships in your life, you won't attract such relationships because you know deep down that it isn't currently true for you. Focus on feeling and nurturing statements that can be spoken as true for you, and focus on your desire as being in process and occurring right now: "I love that I am attracting . . ." or "I feel excited that I am . . ." or "I love the thought of . . . ."

You have formulated a clear desire. You feel fantastic every time you declare it. However, if you have doubt (the uncertainty that you can truly attract your desire to you), that doubt or limiting belief evokes a negative vibration and will cancel out the positive statement of your desire. Eliminate the doubt and rework your desire declaration until it rings true and makes you feel happy and excited.

23

Eliminate Subconscious Doubt

When manifestation takes too long or the Law of Attraction doesn't seem to work as you had hoped, you can assume that there may be blockages or obstacles that need clearing. Check your thought patterns. Are you experiencing skepticism, fear, anxiety, doubt, or worry? Check your feelings. Remedy blockages by asserting control over your conscious mind. Become quiet and permit your higher self or Divine Mind to take charge in quelling your mind's constant chatter.

You can exert control over your conscious thoughts to some degree, but your subconscious may be a wee bit more challenging. You may have the urge to declare that you can't possibly be responsible for any negative thinking that goes on in your subconscious, but the fact is that you are the only one who could possibly be responsible. It is, after all, your mind. Don't blame your parents, ex-wife, or others. Use frequent affirmations and creative visualizations to eliminate doubt and negative emotions that can block your alignment with the workings of the law.

24

Reinforce Your Desire Through Journaling

It is helpful to have a place to record your desire declarations, affirmations, visualizations, statements of evidence or proof, and prayers or statements of gratitude. Include images of your desires and dreams in your journal. As your desires manifest, place a symbol that has meaning for you upon your written declaration. In fact, make a note each time positive things flow easily into your life. Rejoice. When you rejoice and commemorate each manifestation, your vibration aligns with the law to bring you even more abundance.

If you are using personal affirmations, visualizations, and emotional magnetizing of your thoughts and you still feel blocked, try journaling your visualizations. From your visualization exercise, write down everything you observed with your mind's eye. Feel the positive emotions that come up for you when you read over your script. Record all the specific details as well as your feelings. Make your visualization and the journal entry as complete as possible.

Now take time to put everything together. Write, read, and recite a personal desire declaration and an affirmation. Make it true for you. Visualize your desire. Notice your positive emotions. Write about your visualization exercise in your journal. Allow the space in your life for the desire to manifest. When your desire comes into your life, be appreciative and bask in feelings of elation, satisfaction, fulfillment, and gratitude.

25

Identify Your Self-Limiting Thoughts

The first step in modifying self-limiting thoughts is to get rid of old patterns of belief that limit you. Law of Attraction experts assert that limiting beliefs are responsible for your inability to work effectively with the Law of Attraction to creatively and deliberately manifest.

The following exercise can help you identify limiting beliefs that you can then work on releasing. Fill in the blanks. Then make a list of other self-limiting beliefs you have. Rework the negative statements into positive declarations that are true and make you feel good.

- I'd like to start my own business, but I can't because

  _____.

- I would run the Boston Marathon, but I can't because

  _____.

- I would like to buy my own house, but I can't because

  _____.

- If I were just more _____ I could attract my perfect soul mate.

- I wish I could lose weight, but I can't because

  _____.

- Because I don't have a college degree, I am prevented from

  _____.

- I don't dare attempt to _____ because I'm too

  _____.

Years of self-limiting beliefs may be sabotaging you without your realizing it. These beliefs reveal themselves in patterns that keep coming up again and again in your life. For example, you attract the wrong kind of romantic partner: "I can't attract a good man because I always fall for losers, just like my Aunt Milly." Limiting beliefs are often so ingrained that they may seem to be at the heart of who you are, the very core of your being.

Self-limiting beliefs hold you back from most personal and spiritual growth. You may harbor a fear of failure, a fear of never finding Mr. Right, or the fear of success. Perhaps you have engaged in self-sabotage, working hard to achieve something only to undermine your hard work with persistent, self-defeating inner criticism. Or perhaps you have always equated success with "no pain, no gain." With the Law of Attraction, you can have success and abundance, and you do not have to suffer to achieve it. You do have to recognize and release self-limiting beliefs.

If you feel stuck or trapped, set goals for various areas of your life—spiritual, health, family, work, personal. List specific reasons that keep you from reaching your goals, and include what has stopped you in the past. Know that you have the power to release even the most ingrained beliefs, and turn them around into affirmations of unlimited potential.

26

Break Free of Those Self-Limiting Thoughts

Quiet observation of your thoughts will shed light on how much of your inner dialogue is negative in response to internal thoughts or external stimuli. Statements such as "I don't have time," "I can't help it," or "I can't afford it" are self-limiting. You remember an old hurt, and the negative feelings are now there in the present. You see a coat in the department store window and want it, but it costs too much. You feel bad. Such instant, reflexive responses must be subdued and eventually replaced with positive responses.

Author Robert T. Kiyosaki, author of *Rich Dad Poor Dad: What the Rich Teach Their Kids About Money—That the Poor and Middle Class Do Not!*, advises in his books and lectures that people replace the negative, self-limiting phrase "I can't afford it" with the positive question "How can I afford it?"

To create a positive statement for a desire declaration, focus on feeling. For example, "I feel excited that I have all the time I need" or "I am thrilled to know that my talents are in demand in the marketplace and I am attracting the perfect job" or "I am attracting into my life ideal friendships that are vibrant, healthy, nurturing, and stimulating" or "I love feeling abundant and knowing that money easily flows to me from myriad sources." These kinds of declarative statements establish desire linked with positive feelings in the present moment.

27

Clarify and Refine Your Vision If Necessary

The Law of Attraction has no bias and does not differentiate between your positive and negative thoughts. It continually responds to your vibration. Words in a positive affirmation make you feel happy, excited, and anticipatory. When you affirm and visualize your desire for something in positive language and images, your feeling creates a magnetic vibration that draws the desired object into your experience. If your vision begins to feel distant or cloudy at any point, try these two techniques:

1. Fix Visualization Problems

The mind/body connection ensures that you will experience feelings in response to your mental visualization. Let's say you need to attract powerful and influential people into your career path. Consider the imagery you are using to depict them in your mind. If you see powerful people as stern, harsh, and demanding, and bringing into your life more misery, stress, and unreasonable deadlines and responsibilities, you most likely will feel apprehension and dread. Instead, reimagine them as warm, friendly, helpful, generous, and wise associates, perhaps even mentors with a vested interest in helping you advance in your chosen field of endeavor.

2. Eliminate Any Image That Muddies or Confuses Your Vision

Perhaps you dream of having a trim, flexible, and muscular body, but you can't get rid of the extra pounds you gained during a pregnancy. You started a walking program with neighborhood friends and are now eating a healthy, balanced diet, and still the weight clings. In your mind, you see yourself in the bikini you wore at eighteen and you are doing affirmations. Why isn't it working?

The problem is that deep down on a subconscious level, you know you can never be eighteen with that same body again. Try taking a picture of yourself as you look today. Adjust your body size using scissors or a computer tool such as Photoshop. You want to create an image that your mind believes is possible to achieve. Psychological experts say that any time there is a struggle between the conscious and unconscious mind, the unconscious wins. You must convince yourself that a flexible and leaner body is possible for the person you are now. Start with a photo image and make it plausible. Paste that image on your refrigerator, bathroom mirror, and scale. Feel gratitude for each pound or inch lost and find positive ways to reward yourself as the Law of Attraction works with you to create a beautiful, strong, healthy, and leaner body.

28

Clear Blockages

Do you have a fear of success? Are you going through the steps of deliberately manifesting and yet not seeing results? Perhaps you are subconsciously blocking the outcome you seek. Try these six steps to clear blockages:

1. **Cultivate positive feelings.** Imagine you have just received whatever it was that you hoped to manifest. Using that moment as a point of departure in a journal entry, write about how you feel at having that object, situation, or relationship now manifested in your life. Remember that the Law of Attraction responds to feelings around specific thoughts rather than the thoughts themselves.

2. **Feel worthy.** Redirect negative self-talk into positive statements. What are some of the reasons why other people (for example, your mother, father, spouse, lover, and children) love you? Make a list of all the lovable qualities and traits you have, and why you are worthy to receive the gifts you seek from the universe. Love yourself and others the way you want to be loved, and cultivate feelings of self-worth.

3. **Make every day the best day of your life.** If something goes wrong in your day, shift the energy of that moment as soon as possible. Don't go through an entire day with a negative attitude. Listen to beautiful music, get physical and take a walk, lie down for a quick power nap, rejuvenate and refresh by doing some yoga or breath work, listen to a Law of Attraction CD, or offer a prayer of thanks to the Divine. You have phenomenal power in every moment of your life to change that moment, to shift the negative into neutral or positive energy, and to regain forward impetus.

4. **Focus on what you want rather than what you don't have.** Perhaps you can easily recount all the reasons why you don't own your own home, but you deeply desire to own a house. Make a list of all

the positive reasons why you deserve it, and how living there will change your life and the lives of your spouse, children, and pets. As a point of departure for writing about your hopes and dreams and feelings of love and gratitude, imagine a celebratory meal with relatives, a holiday gathering, or a quiet peaceful moment in your own home. Take a mental snapshot of how you feel after that writing exercise. Remember those positive feelings every time you move into feelings of lack.

5. **Fine-tune the direction and intention of your desires.** Be decisive when working with the law. Remember that it is always at work to bring you the things you mentally focus on, both positive and negative. Think of your mind as a canoe floating along the river of life, buffeted and buoyed by forces of energy (wind and currents) that you can't see. For certain, that canoe is going somewhere, perhaps places you like or don't. Instead of going with the flow, remember that you have the power to navigate the direction you desire to go in through the paddles of your feelings and thoughts.

6. **Create space in your life for what you desire to manifest.** Consider that the new love of your life might not come until your current relationship has ended. If there is a lot of negative emotional baggage associated with the relationship you are in, you have to clear out those patterns of thought and replace them with positive feelings of anticipatory excitement, hope, and expectation that your clear and determined focus is attracting to you the new love you desire and deserve.

29

Support Your Intention with Dream Incubation

Dream work can inspire, enlighten, and amuse you, even if you have never done it before. The most important thing besides remembering your dreams is to know how to incubate a dream for understanding, insight, and guidance. When you are working with the Law of Attraction in an intentional way, you may find it helpful to incubate a dream to clarify whether you are on your path or are obstructing the manifestation of something you deeply desire, or for guidance on how to turbo-charge your intention to get what you want.

- Place a pad of paper and a pencil next to your bed. Even better, purchase and use a dream journal (any blank book will do).
- Upon awakening, remain in that sleepy state and notice how you feel from having that dream. Try to recall all the images you can about your dream.
- Without judging or analyzing your dream, write everything you can remember about the dream, especially your feeling and mood as you awakened.
- After you have recorded your dream, consult a good dream dictionary to choose meanings for the symbols that make sense to you.
- Once you have interpreted all the symbols, actions, messages, themes, and any particularly potent images, rewrite the dream to expose its relevance and meaning. Meaning can be revealed in the layers of the dream or even over a period of time during which you dream the same dream again, so consult books about dream work to learn how to extract as much meaning as possible.

Incubating a dream requires a little preparation. Before going to sleep, do some breath work. As you breathe out, visualize dark negative energy that you've acquired during the day flowing out through the soles of your feet beyond the horizon line. As you breathe in, visualize white light or positive energy flowing in through your heart or head and filling your body. Ask for the dream you desire. Be clearly focused and specific—for example, "I open my heart and mind to receiving a dream about _____." Here are three techniques for dream incubation:

1. Prepare and pray for the dream. Ask your dreaming mind for exactly what you want. Don't try to incubate a dream after consuming heavy food or drink. Likewise, avoid incubating a dream when you are extremely tired or grumpy or overstimulated by work or conversations with friends. Take a hot shower or bath to wind down from your day. Make certain your bedroom is clean with fresh linen on the bed. You should feel peaceful and ready to sleep. Ensure that you have placed the necessary tools for recording your dream close by.

2. Fantasize and explore every aspect of your dream topic until you can write out a short one-sentence dream question or goal. During a meditation or quiet period, think about every aspect of the type of information you require or desire to receive from the dream. Clarity of what you seek and how you feel about what you seek to discover is essential.

3. Open your heart and mind to any and all possibilities for information your dream (or dreams) may bring you about the topic in question. Understand that sometimes your dreaming mind may offer the dream in different ways on different nights. In essence, your dreaming mind brings you the information you desire sequentially, as if it were a flower slowly unfolding and yielding its secrets.

30

Promote Good Health with Healthy Thinking

If you want to get healthy and stay that way, start with healthy thoughts. Here are some questions to ask yourself about your current state of health.

- Think about how you felt at a time when you were at the peak of good health. Ask yourself what brought about the decline in your health. Is it something that can remain in the past or is it still a factor? If it is still a factor, what can you do to get rid of it or minimize its impact?
- How committed are you to improving your health, stamina, and overall well-being?
- What steps will you take in the next moment, hour, or day to get on the road to good health?

Remember, poor overall health can attract other problems and even shorten your life expectancy. Could you be bringing on your own illnesses or attracting misfortune in your life through the power of negative thought? If so, doesn't it make sense that changing your thoughts could change your life for the better?

The Tibetan Buddhist approach to healing necessarily begins in the mind. The Buddhist philosophy teaches that the mind is the creator of all problems and remedies, good fortune and bad, health and sickness. Buddhists believe in the Law of Karma. Each person is constantly sowing karmic seeds that persist until the right circumstances occur to cause the seeds to bear their karmic fruit. Negative karma manifests as problems, disease, and suffering, while positive karma shows up as success, good fortune, and vibrant health. To the degree that you can control your emotions and thought patterns, you can influence your karma and, thus, your health and vitality.

31

Stimulate Your Mind with New Challenges

People working deliberately with the Law of Attraction may gain increased benefit from focusing on their health because of their optimistic outlook for improving their conditions. Andrew Weil, MD, a leading expert on integrative medicine and author of a plethora of books about health, asserts that maintaining a healthy mind is equally important. Find ways to engage your mind in interesting endeavors. A healthy mind is an engaged mind in a healthy body. For example, your mind is stimulated when you endeavor to learn how to speak a new language, play a musical instrument, and do crossword or sudoku puzzles. A healthy mind also focuses on positive rather than negative thought patterns. Perhaps you have noticed in your own life a link between periods of positive thought patterns and feelings of wellness versus negative thinking and maladies.

You can also use sound healing, aromatherapy, massage, breath work, herbal and hydro therapies, and guided meditation for mind/body healing. They are techniques found in virtually every medical tradition, including the ancient health teachings of Ayurveda, and increasingly Western-trained physicians may include those therapies along with medications and other conventional treatments.

32

Set Boundaries and Resolve Conflicts

Working with the Law of Attraction goes hand in hand with healthy conflict resolution. How? When you cannot establish firm boundaries or say no to others' demands, you may feel that people such as coaches, friends, business associates, or family members are treading all over you. As a result, you may harbor feelings of hostility and resentment. That hostility can create stress and distraction that can deter or delay your intentions. Use the following techniques to reduce your stress and anxiety while resolving conflicts with others.

1. Stay focused on the present situation and be in tune with your mood and vibration. When your vibration is high and you feel good, you are in tune with the Law of Attraction and can more easily draw in a healthy solution to a conflict.

2. Concentrate on regular, slow breathing to help you remain calm, clear-thinking, and able to make good choices.

3. Attempt to truly understand the other person's point of view.

4. Show restraint when accusations and criticism are leveled at you, and respond with empathy for how the speaker is feeling.

5. Make it clear that you will work with him to find a solution.

6. Actively listen and avoid the tendency to interrupt or anticipate what the other person might say next.

7. Take responsibility for your words, attitude, and actions. If you are wrong, own up to it and release it.

8. Avoid defensive posturing.

9. Seek a compromise. If agreement cannot be reached, involve an impartial third party to help you resolve the conflict.

10. Request a break if the discussion has become too heated and the communication is no longer constructive. Agree to resume it later at a specific time after you've both had time to allow any aggressive feelings and anger to dissipate.

Set aside a little time every day to release the cumulative stressful feelings you have taken on throughout your day. Release the tension. Put on some quiet music or sit or lie quietly and just be aware of your breath. Let go of tension with every outgoing breath. Feel appreciation and joy for the gift of life and for a functioning body that is your vehicle for this incarnation. Be grateful in the knowledge that it is in your power to create vibrant health.

33

Give in Order to Receive

Giving what you desire to manifest more of it in your life is an important concept. If you want money, give money; if you want love or respect, then show love and respect to others. If you are stingy in your giving, then don't be surprised if only a little money trickles back. Your gift, however, is less important than your attitude about living an abundant life—giving and believing that you will always have more to give. Of itself, that is a powerful positive affirmation.

Here's a simple way to give: If you go to the grocery store and see a bell ringer for charity standing outside when you leave, throw some money in the bucket. Mentally affirm that the money will return to you many times over to help you build financial prosperity for yourself and your family.

Another tip: According to feng shui experts, placing a water fountain that can run twenty-four hours each day in the prosperity area of a room (located in the rear left corner as you stand in the doorway looking in) will stimulate the positive flow of money. Financial abundance will begin to circulate around you just as the water circulates around the fountain.

34

Adopt the Millionaire Mindset

Financial success comes even more quickly when you do the following three things: imagine your monetary desire with strong intention to manifest it; frequently focus purposeful attention on your goals; and be actively involved in achieving your desired outcome. Be on the lookout and take advantage of new opportunities to create income streams and remain open to allowing the universe to bring you what you want.

Millionaires have something in common besides wealth. Here are some of the habits and beliefs that wealthy people share:

- When something doesn't work, they don't view it as a failure so much as an opportunity to learn how not to behave, so that during their next effort they are successful.
- They do not give up even before they've started.
- They use their money wisely.
- They take responsibility for what happens in their life and do not believe that things happen by chance.
- They have respect for others and will enlist help from others to ensure the success of an endeavor.
- Regardless of the potential for a negative (even disastrous) result in a situation, they will always look for the possible positive outcome.
- They believe strongly in the necessity of commitment, not only to others but to the project.
- They do not engage in self-limiting thoughts, and instead of saying "I can't afford it," they will ask "How can I afford it?"

Think about the word "money" for a moment and see what kind of emotional responses the term evokes in you. Do you have negative feelings about never having enough of it? Do you view having money as not compatible with your spiritual life? Your thoughts about abundance or lack of money create a vibration that magnetizes your mindset. That magnetic vibration either impedes or enhances the flow of currency to you.

35

Get Out of Debt and Manifest Prosperity

Failure and lack in life are manifested first in the mind. Somehow you imagined lack and it found you. So how do you get out from under the weight of debt to manifest financial prosperity?

One fun way to focus your energy is to make a wealth poster. On the center of a poster board, place or draw something that symbolizes the infinite source—for example, the infinity symbol (the number eight lying on its side). Around the perimeter, write the areas of your life, such as relationships, knowledge, and health. Add images and affirmations to symbolize the things you desire for each area and how money will help you achieve those desires.

As you discuss your financial situation, avoid using the words "debt" and "bill." Those words are supercharged with negativity. If you try to formulate a positive affirmation such as "I am happy that I'm getting out of debt," the subconscious will key in on the word *debt* and bring you more. Ditto for the word *bill*. It is far better to write out an affirmation that excludes those two words. For example, "I am happy that my money increases every day and that I can now pay off my car." Or, "I am overjoyed that my wealth is growing daily, and I can easily make my mortgage payment with plenty of money left over."

If you spend even a little time reverting back to old patterns of thought about how little money you really have and how your financial obligations are so numerous that you may never get out of debt, you are sabotaging any positive efforts you may be making to attract money. Stay focused on what you want. Give your emotional and thought energy to that.

36

Make a Wealth Receptacle

Infuse this exercise with enthusiasm, happiness, and a sense of expectation, for completing it can help you focus on wealth and potential avenues (such as jobs or businesses) to generate it.

1. Find and decorate a tray, urn, hat box, coffee can, or some other receptacle in red and gold, colors that attract prosperity.

2. On a piece of paper, write out your declarations for wealth, making them clear and succinct and including the time frame during which you want your wealth to manifest.

3. Put the paper containing your wealth desires into a red envelope and drop it into the box.

4. Add other items that symbolize your wealth desires.

5. Place the box near a money tree plant and a small bubbling fountain or aquarium. Finally, place a small lamp or other light source with a red bulb in that sector. (If you are practicing feng shui, place the box in the wealth sector of your home or office.)

In every culture, when people want to manifest something in their life expression, they often surround themselves with images of the things they desire to manifest. Symbolically, the items you place in highly visible areas stimulate your mind to turn toward thoughts of prosperity.

In your wealth receptacle or container, you could add a miniature statue of the Money Buddha or Lakshmi, the Hindu goddess of wealth. Other possibilities include the tarot deck's Ace of Pentacles since it represents wealth, money, luck, and the successful beginning of a new business or enterprise. You might add old Chinese feng shui coins—obtain them from a wealthy place, not one going out of business—or dollar bills in multiples of the number eight. Eight is such a lucky number for wealth that in China, businessmen strive to get that number in their addresses and phone numbers. It is believed to double their incomes.

You could also drop in a piece of jade, a semiprecious stone believed to attract good luck and fortune. If you think there may be obstacles in your path to wealth, install a small statue of the Hindu god Ganesh, the remover of obstacles. Hang a gold-colored wind chime from which are strung metal cylinders and Chinese coins. The movement of the chiming elements suggests the attraction and circulation of money. Light a red candle.

If you are endeavoring to attract prosperity, avoid spending money you don't have. Don't expect that you'll go to sleep at night and find your wallet will be miraculously full of currency when you awake in the morning. Watch for the means of prosperity to suddenly start showing up in your life as job offers or business connections, alliances, and new opportunities. At first, they may seem like coincidences or synchronicity at work. Record the proof of the Law of Attraction at work by noting in your journal, diary, or scheduling book whenever you find a penny, get a gift certificate you didn't expect, receive a free coffee at Starbucks, notice a forgotten five-dollar bill in the pocket of a jacket you picked up at a yard sale, or see some other sign that the law is at work in your life.

37

Celebrate Milestones on Your Journey

Aristotle noted roughly 2,300 years ago that humans seek happiness more than anything else. When you feel happy and fulfilled, you know you are on track. Conversely, when you feel dissatisfied and unhappy, you are off track.

Aligned with the Law of Attraction, you will find actualizing a dream to be easier than perhaps you believed possible. When you are on your path in life, living the way you feel passionate about, the law, like wind in the sail of a boat, pushes powerfully forward and causes impediments to float away. Here are some tips to try:

- Take stock of what every aspect of your dream looks like. Journaling works wonders for fleshing out your ideas.
- Believe in your dream, follow your passion, and don't let anyone talk you out it.
- Notice the obstacles, especially family, friends, and associates who are naysayers. Remove the obstacles and find a way to navigate around the people.
- If you can't do the endeavor alone, surround yourself with the best people you can find, especially if they are smarter or have more experience than you.
- Be prepared to make your own rules if you have to. Sometimes there are no other good options.
- Establish a timeline and stick to it.
- Celebrate the milestones to encourage your forward momentum.

Believe that you deserve the best. Enjoy getting it. When you are on track in your job, life, or personal relationships, you exude happiness.

Regain Good Health with This Breathing Exercise

The following breathing technique has been practiced by yogis for centuries. Breathing techniques were known by the ancients and have been used in many cultures either alone or with herbs or other elements to restore balance in the body for health. If you feel ill, try the following breathing exercise.

- Sitting in a comfortable position with straight posture, place your right thumb against your right nostril. Breathe in through the left nostril slowly until your lungs are full.
- Release the thumb and press the first finger of the same hand against the left nostril and breathe out through the right.
- Inhale through the right nostril, then close it off and breathe out through the left.
- Repeat the cycle three to five times. (Yogis advocated doing this exercise before sunrise, at noon, at sunset, and at midnight to achieve purity of the nervous system for spiritual practice.)
- When you feel calm and rebalanced, relax and resume normal breathing. Visualize your body's soldiers (white blood cells) proliferating and gathering in a specific area that is in need of healing, or circulating throughout the body if you are trying to heal something like the flu. Feel the breaking up of tension in the afflicted area and warmth filling it. Visualize the healing.

In working with the Law of Attraction, you need not dwell on what initially caused the problem nor worry about when the condition initially emerged. Your work is to believe that the condition or illness is gone and vibrant health has returned.

39

Attract the Perfect Romantic Partner

The Law of Attraction will bring someone perfect for you if you allow for that to happen in your life. Be aware that you cannot change anyone but yourself, so don't try to use the law for that purpose. It won't work because you don't own their vibration and thoughts. You can change only yourself.

Focus on the life you want with the kind of person you want. Feel joy, gratitude, and peace to raise your vibration to draw that person to you. You have a choice in every moment to be available to love. Put your attention there and the attraction begins. Don't worry about when, where, or how it will happen. Know that someone special is en route to you at this moment. The speed of the arrival is directly related to the strength and magnetism of your thoughts, intention, and desire.

Make a list of the good qualities you seek in a partner and why. Or, if it's easier, list the qualities you don't want and then use each in a sentence that states the opposite, or the quality you do want. For example, this could be a negative statement: "I feel insulted and disrespected when I hear profanity carelessly peppered throughout my date's vocabulary." Think about the opposite and use it to write a positive statement: "I feel happy, loved, and respected when my date is thoughtful and considerate about word choices."

40

Recognize Synchronicity

Swiss psychologist Carl Jung coined the term *synchronicity*. Many people have experienced coincidences in their lives, but when such events are multiple and meaningful, synchronicity is surely at work. Some people believe that the more a person evolves, the more synchronicity occurs in her life. Others suggest that synchronous events happen because of excitable emotion and a strong expectation that draws such occurrences into manifestation.

Synchronicity is one indicator that the Law of Attraction is at work and that something you have asked for is beginning to make its way to you. It bears repeating that it is worthwhile to pay attention to coincidences. Watch for evidence of meaningful occurrences and their connectivity. Notice patterns of flow, when things easily happen or come together. Observe how little signs begin to show up and give notice that the universe has received your request.

You may not notice it, but synchronicity is going on all the time. Learn to live your life in a magical yet purposeful way, and you'll begin to see the meaningful—even mystical—occurrences in life that you may be missing because you are distracted or too busy or tired to notice. Synchronicities are those little meaningful coincidences that can point you in new directions or provide you with moments of breakthrough understanding. The more you notice them, the more of them, seemingly, there are to notice.

41

Foster Spiritual Growth

Maybe you desire to dive deeper in meditation than you have ever gone. Perhaps you want to replace a bad habit with a good one that better serves your spiritual endeavors. Maybe you seek inspiration for meaningful spiritual work you can do to benefit the world, or you seek a teacher or inspiration for the direction to take on your personal spiritual path. You can do all those things and even more by deliberate and intentional work with the Law of Attraction.

The Law of Attraction works whether you nurture the divine within and seek increase for your spiritual life, or whether you do things that evoke the law of decrease. When you criticize others, demean a person's choices, devalue someone's work, or spread gossip about someone, you are setting in motion three universal laws: the Law of Decrease, the Law of Karma, and the Law of Attraction. Don't waste your mental currency on such negative activity since it will return to you in kind. Instead, focus on working with the Law of Increase and the Law of Attraction to manifest spiritual results.

The goal of spiritual evolution, according to many New Age spiritual seekers, is to arrive at the following realization: That which you seek, you already are. As a child of the Divine, all of creation is your playground. You can do and have whatever you desire. In tune with the wisdom of your heart, be ever conscious that you are a spark of the Great Light. Let love flow unimpeded from your heart. Remember the counsel of Rumi: "Let the beauty we love be what we do."

Detach Yourself from Outcomes

Knowing that you can create any dream from the field of infinite potentiality, you can let go of attachment to the outcome. For some people, the notion of detachment may be a little more difficult to grasp. It doesn't mean you have to let go of your intention to manifest something. Attachment to the outcome might mean, for example, that you hoped for a new car and you expected a Volkswagen, but a Ferrari showed up. Are you going to complain to the Universe that the Ferrari was not acceptable? Are you that attached to having a Volkswagen? Unlikely.

You wanted money to start flowing into your life and expected it to come when you won a promotion, but you won the lotto instead. Are you going to be disappointed at how the money came? Let go of trying to micromanage the Universe's work and force a particular outcome. Instead, cultivate a deep abiding conviction in your true self's power to create anything you need, want, or desire, and let the outcome of your belief, desire, and endeavor bear fruit.

43

Be Patient

When you do spiritual work, you must surrender and listen to the voice within. Surrendering to that inner wisdom allows you to know with a kind of understanding that goes beyond logical thinking. Likewise, when you work with the Law of Attraction, you must set aside logic and reason. Cultivate trust and faith, and know with an inner certainty that the law works. When the law gives you even a little indication that it is working, you will feel excited and your belief will be reaffirmed. Your excitement increases your joyful vibration, which, in turn, increases your level of trust in the law.

Working with the Law of Attraction requires letting go of the need to control the time frame during which your desire manifests. Trust that the universe is doing what's necessary to bring about your intention. As the noted psychologist Carl Rogers once observed, "You can't push the river."

The Law of Attraction works with momentum. Things can manifest instantly or take a long time to unfold. Why? A lot has to do with the strength of your desire, the clarity of your vision, and the power of your intention. The universe is rearranging itself to bring you what you want. It also allows you to wrangle with your choice and all the different aspects, elements, and options your mind conceives.

Find Solutions to Your Problems

Sometimes when you are on a spiritual path, life issues and problems begin to surface unexpectedly, even frequently. Some yogis assert that this happens because you are consciously making efforts at spiritual unfolding and this speeds up processes that make your karmic debts and gifts show up more quickly.

You can overthink or overanalyze a problem and block ideas for possible options. Your brain is constantly bombarded with information and must work like a processor to deal with it all. Think of meditation as a period of relief for the brain. In a calm yet alert and focused state, ideas will begin to flow.

Regular daily meditation, even if you only do it for ten minutes or so, offers a period of relief from life's constant barrage of stimulation and problems. When you meditate, you temporarily shut off the senses, calm your breathing, and allow your brain to rest and recharge. Then an amazing thing happens. After a period of inner stillness when you again bring mental focus upon a problem, solutions may pop into your mind. Such options may be ones you never thought of because your hyperfocus on the problem blocked them.

You can also bring about an energy shift by doing something physical. Leave your problem at the house or office and take a walk outside. The energy vibration of nature can calm you. Not thinking about the problem while you enjoy a stroll around a lake, through the woods, on the beach, around a park, or across a meadow clears and refreshes your mind. The Law of Attraction, as you know, is always at work. When you detach from the problems, knowing with deep conviction that inherent in every problem is the means to solve it, the law can effortlessly deliver a solution.

45

Recover Quickly from Bad Moods

The Law of Attraction responds to emotional shifts up and down. Depression, anger, and sadness are stark contrasts to joy, love, and happiness. Dark feelings function as radar. They signal that your thoughts have turned negative. To return to a positive mood, you have to shift your thoughts until your feelings begin to shift.

Your power to shift emotion up and down by your thoughts means you can live your life from the inside out with the knowledge of how to deliberately attract the good things in life. You'll have greater satisfaction as you work with your own thoughts and emotions to directly experience your true self and divine purpose in life. Finally, you will have the knowledge and experience to work with the universal laws to create virtually anything.

You shift from being confrontational to feeling joyful by:

- Removing yourself from the situation and triggers
- Breathing slowly to calm your agitation and help you release the anger
- Listening to beautiful music
- Forgiving
- Thinking of a pleasant memory and allowing your mind to move into the positive emotions associated with that experience

Find Your Ideal Job

If you are employed by a company in a job that does not feel right, but you need the paycheck and have no good options for moving to another employer, consider working with the Law of Attraction to inspire and guide you to a new position in your current company. Until you can locate another potential place of employment, you have to think of what to do from where you currently are. It may mean staying in the dead-end job until exit is possible. Don't be disheartened. Plant the seeds of desire and intent today so that the universe can rearrange itself to give you that new job.

Begin thinking about your dream job and how passionate you feel doing it. If that job doesn't exist, don't give up. Create that ideal job by imagining it. Envision everything associated with your ideal job. Tailor your desires. Be specific. Refine. Just the thought of being able to achieve your goals increases clarity and determination. What type of work is it? What tasks are you required to do? What does the office building look like? Who are the other workers (for example, are they highly skilled international workers or highly diverse college-age whiz kids)? What are the work hours/schedule? How much money do you make? What is your title? Can you see yourself owning the company?

47

Practice Using Your Intuition

Regardless of what you call it—intuition, sixth sense, instinct—to some degree, everyone has the ability to sense things. By practicing relaxation and calming of the mind, you clear out the mental clutter and quiet the chattering to allow your intuition to bring forth innovative ideas, solutions, and concepts to help you meet professional business goals and get results.

Learn to rely on your emotional guidance system of intuition or sixth sense to know when to let go. If something is not right in your life, you may be overriding the signals from your emotional guidance system that warn you to steer clear or break away. The more you rely on your inner guidance, the more you will trust it when it warns you to shift direction. Sometimes just a little shift is all that is needed to create a vacuum for financial prosperity and the abundance that you may seek.

48

Get a Raise or Promotion

The secret to working with the Law of Attraction to manifest a raise or promotion is to create a powerful, compelling mental video that excites you every time you play it in your mind. To get the raise you want, see yourself meeting with the person empowered to grant the raise. Think, act, and speak during the meeting as if the raise has already been approved. Feel the elation of knowing that your next paycheck will include that money. Imagine how you will use it.

Use affirmations, visualizations, journal writing, and poster-making projects to intentionally reprogram your thoughts to accept that you have been given the raise. See this as your business plan for getting what you desire from your career.

Use the same process for manifesting a promotion. See yourself in your mental video receiving the news that your promotion has come through. See yourself at a company meeting where your promotion is announced. Now play the video forward to hear the high praises your boss shares about you and your work with others attending your celebration party. Feel all the positive emotions associated with being in your new elevated position.

49

Employ Feng Shui to Keep Your Home's Energy Flowing

Take stock of your home to ascertain whether clutter blocks easy navigation through the entry and all areas of the house. Is the home painted and furnished in a way that creates a warm welcome? Has your love of furniture overfilled rooms so that they feel crowded and cramped?

You influence the flow of the life-affirming chi throughout your surroundings by the way you incorporate physical objects and plants in the interior as well as by your color choices, furniture and art placement, interior lighting, art objects, and symbolic items representing nature.

When rooms are stuffed, the flow of energy is blocked and can become stagnant. Your goal is to ensure that there are open pathways through your home to allow the energy passage. When the energy can freely swirl around your environment (and by feng shui association, every area of your life), your good fortune or luck changes along with your power to intentionally attract what you desire.

There are several ways to improve energy flow and establish a balance of masculine and feminine elements (yin/yang). For example, you could add some healthy plants, a judicious splash of contrast color, objects to represent nature, and some good illumination to let the chi flow easily. You will know that the chi is moving through that space because you will feel happy, harmonious, healthy, calm, peaceful, and relaxed. Those positive feelings associated with flowing chi are exactly the positive feelings that aid the work of the Law of Attraction in bestowing abundance in your life.

The point of feng shui is to create an energetically balanced space that supports you and your life choices, that invites you, friends, and family members into a sense of community. The interior space in which feng shui is properly used fosters the flow of energy that is correct for the function of that space. In a bedroom, the energy will be grounded and safe, harmonious, and peaceful. A living room, on the other hand, might have more lively energy flowing through it. The energy in that space encourages acceptance, love, safety, and grounding, but with a smidgen of risk as represented by the use of a splash of vibrant color, a precariously placed object, or a piece of visual art depicting something wildly imaginative in bold line and color.

Eliminate Clutter

Clutter suppresses and even obstructs energy flow. Stagnant or blocked energy or chi makes your life difficult. Sapped of energy, your health suffers. Stagnant energy also blocks the flow of money. It impedes the manifestation of healthy relationships. It obstructs advancements in your chosen career path. It can bring on depression and negative patterns of thought.

Organize a particular room or area of your home or office. Once that area is completed, tackle the next room and the next until the whole house is re-energized. Baskets (symbolizing the reeds and grasses of nature) with lids are great for organizing objects in a room that were carried in and forgotten. Left to pile up, they begin to slow down or block the natural flow of energizing chi.

Have piles of books been there so long that you had forgotten about them and don't even see them when you enter the room? Are there piles of books, dead or dying plants, a couch, chair, or table with loose screws or broken legs? Since these things represent bad feng shui, there's a pretty good chance your health is being affected. Have you noticed feeling fatigued, drained, stressed, or unhappy? Such symptoms indicate an imbalance in the energy of your home.

In *Feng Shui Living*, Sharon Stasney noted that accumulation and letting go is actually part of an ancient yin/yang cycle. The yin part of the cycle is the accumulation of items while the yang portion is the letting go of those things. In the Law of Attraction, this is akin to making space in your life for something to manifest.

To fix that room, remove any broken or damaged items. Take away or organize and store objects of clutter. Bring in fresh flowers, aesthetically pleasing pictures, and objects of art in the healing colors of nature. Add an accent in the color of green (earth) and gold (sun), two powerful elements of nature that are both necessary for a healthy life-giving energy.

Eliminate Clutter

51

Use Pendulum Dowsing to Know If You Are On Track

Pendulum dowsing has been around for thousands of years. Recently it has gained acceptance as a divining tool to help determine if a person is on the right track for drawing in the things he wants with the Law of Attraction. The pendulum can give yes/no answers. One of the earliest dowsing images dates to circa 6000 B.C.

Pendulums 101

Through history, pendulums have been used to find water, precious metals, gems, oil, and gas as well as lost people, lost objects, ghosts, and negative earth energies. Pendulums are made of a piece of string, cord, or chain with some kind of weight handing from one end. The object with weight can be made of almost anything that is not magnetized—a key, wooden bead, paperclip, ring, metal fishing weight, quartz crystal, or glass ball, or even a Chinese coin with a square hole often used in feng shui—that can freely swing from a lightweight cord or chain. Cord length ranges from around nine to fifteen inches, whatever is most comfortable for you.

Prepare Yourself and Your Space

To use the pendulum for dowsing or divining answers, you must enter a state of calm alertness. If you do not know how to calm yourself and become relaxed while entering a state of clear focus, try the following. First, take a warm bath, perhaps with some aromatherapy oil. The point is to let go of the stresses of the day and to become grounded, centered, and focused.

Dress in comfortable clothes and sit in a softly lit area, perhaps with fresh flowers, a glass of water, and peaceful instrumental music. Breathe deeply to release any remaining tension in the body. Once you are fully relaxed, offer a prayer to the Divine. Offer heartfelt thanks every time you engage in pendulum dowsing. You may then drink the water or pour it onto a living plant such as lucky bamboo or a money plant, as it becomes magnetized by your spiritual vibrations.

Suspend Your Pendulum

To work with the pendulum, suspend the cord with its weighted object by looping a bit of excess cord or chain over your index finger. An alternative technique is to use a bead at one end of the chain and a heavier object, such as a crystal, at the other end. Place the bead between your index and middle finger of your dominant hand, allowing the string or chain with the crystal to dangle vertically to about an inch from the open palm of your other hand.

The pendulum and chain should feel so natural that it is like part of you, your arm, and your hand. The pendulum will swing back and forth, in circles, and/or side to side, hovering just above the open palm of your bottom hand. Picture your open palms facing each other and you will have the correct position.

Determining Dates and Time

The pendulum works through the force of your intuition or sixth sense. Some people use the pendulum to find out the hour or date something will happen. For such questions, it is helpful to draw on paper a circular clock with the increments marked, or use a calendar with the dates and days in squares over which you can swing the pendulum. For example, you might ask which date in August would be best to start your summer vacation. Swing the pendulum over the days you are considering and see if it gives you a sign (downward pull or wildly swinging over one of the dates).

You can get simple yes or no answers if you phrase the questions carefully. Consider asking questions like "Would the beginning of August be better than the end?" "Would the first week be better than the second?" "Would a weekday be better than a weekend?"

Testing Accuracy

When you are ready to start working with the pendulum, establish your ground rules. Tell your higher self or your angels or guides that a clockwise circle indicates a yes answer and a counter-clockwise indicates a no. Show them by deliberately swinging the pendulum in each of those directions. Ask them to show you when they are ready by demonstrating a yes response. Watch the pendulum start to swing in a clockwise circular pattern. When it does, thank them for demonstrating that they are present and ready. Ask your first question.

To test the accuracy of your pendulum, intermittently ask questions for which you already know the answer, such as "Is my name Murgatroyd?" You know the answer is no and the pendulum should swing in a counter-clockwise circular pattern, according to the rules you've established.

Many pendulum users also ask to be shown what a maybe response looks like. It may be a forty-five-degree movement, side to side, or some other pattern distinctively different from the circular yes and no patterns.

Don't Second-Guess the Answers

Don't doubt or second-guess or rationalize the answers you may receive when you work with the pendulum. Doing so impedes or blocks the energy from your higher self just as surely as clutter blocks the vital energy swirling through an environment.

Working with the Law of Attraction, you know that the self-limiting thoughts and the criticisms and self-doubt will limit your effectiveness. When you work with the pendulum, let go of doubt. Trust the truth of the information you receive.

One way to validate the information you receive through pendulum dowsing is to keep a journal of the questions you ask and the responses you get when you pendulum-dowse for answers to help you with decisions. Later on, you can read how many answers were correctly given. This will also inspire you to seek answers about your life that will keep you moving forward in a positive direction.

52

Strengthen Your Self-Care

One of the most vital aspects of working with the Law of Attraction requires that you take care of yourself. Self-care begins with self-nourishment and self-acceptance. Only when you have these things will you find meaning in all the other things you desire to attract. A million dollars won't mean much if you are too ill to spend it. The love of your life can show up, but if you aren't emotionally healthy enough to receive him or her, the relationship won't satisfy you for long.

Love Yourself

Love yourself as though you were showing love to your spouse or lover. If you've just broken up with someone, turn all the love that you were sending toward the other person back upon yourself. When you are in love, you have energy to spare. You are happy, perhaps obsessively so, as you consider doing special things for that special someone. Do those things for yourself.

Notice Apathy

If you don't move your body, it simply won't work as well. Your muscles begin to shrink. Flexibility lessens along with your range of motion. You start to gain weight. That won't make you feel good about yourself. Life becomes dull. It seems to take a lot of effort to just get motivated to go through your day. It's a snowball effect; things go from bad to worse. Until you shift the energy and start down a different path to becoming fully alive and engaged in your life, the Law of Attraction will continue bringing you the same old stuff.

53

Allow Manifestation to Occur

Perhaps the most important step in deliberate manifestation is the art of allowing something to come into your life. Believe that you deserve it, are worthy, and ready to receive. Let your desire come in. In the twelve-step program there is an admonishment to "let go, and let God." It's that simple. When you allow, you feel relief and other positive emotions.

Simply allow for the manifestation to arrive in its own perfect time. The process of it coming to you should be the focus rather than achieving the object, according to practitioners of *wu-wei,* as the art of effortlessly manifesting is known.

PART 3

Finding Happiness

You can now draw to yourself a brighter future, vibrant health, transformational thinking, financial prosperity, abundance of every kind, and deeper and more profound spiritual connections. You have risen above the fetters that have been holding you back through self-limiting thought to discover the world anew. You have allowed your newfound sense of wonder to inspire feelings of gratitude. But what if, after you have attracted to you everything you ever dreamed of, emotion still tugs at your heart? Perhaps it's your sense of altruism asking you to give as generously as you've received.

CHAPTER 5

Share the Knowledge

CREATE BETTER LIVES BY TEACHING OTHERS

When you began to put the Law of Attraction to work in your life, did you begin to keep a journal noting the dates and times when the law gave you exactly what you asked for and when it manifested? Such documentation can serve not only as validation but also as future inspiration as you continue working with the law. You have learned the secret power of co-creation in harmony and gratitude with the Divine. Now it's your turn to share your knowledge, experience, insights, and enthusiasm with others.

You know people who are always complaining that they can't get ahead in life no matter what they do. They are the walking wounded. They may have lost jobs, be in pain, or be at risk of losing their homes. They may wonder if they are living under some kind of curse. At church, they find comfort in hearing that God loves them, watches over them, and can help them, but they don't know how to help themselves. These are people you can teach to avail themselves of financial prosperity, joy, and success in every area of life.

You can also learn from them. Questions and comments posed by others inevitably provide different lenses for examining a subject. Sharing knowledge is often a two-way flow. Teaching someone else something is a sure-fire method for learning more about it yourself.

Different Types of Leaders

Leaders, whether in organizations or businesses, motivate people. But no two leaders are exactly alike in their style and approach. Some leaders use negative motivational tools such as intimidation, fear, and ridicule and, consequently, find that these hurtful tactics usually only work in the short-term, and can backfire. Positive motivation not only helps people help themselves, but it can also function as self-motivation for leaders.

The Taoist Lao Tzu once said that if you give a man a fish, he eats for a day. But if you teach the man to fish, he can eat for the rest of his life. The point is not to promote another person's reliance upon you to keep providing the fish, but to empower that individual to find the sustenance from life on his own. When he understands how to manifest his heart's many desires and his body's assorted needs in alliance with the Law of Attraction, he will be able to sustain himself without your intervention. That is not to say you can't emotionally and psychologically support him and others.

ENOUGH FOR EVERYONE

A common question that pops up in conversations about the Law of Attraction is that if everyone gets to have as much abundance in their lives as they want, will it take something away from others? The answer is no. The world of formless energy and substance out of which all of creation takes shape is boundless and limitless. It's not a scale that tips when weight is added or rises when something is removed. Perceiving the truth that an abundant life is available for all may require a new way of thinking for some people.

SEEING BEYOND DUALITY

Enlightened beings from ancient times to the present day have said that the creation of the universe (or multiverse, for those who believe that there could be infinite universes) occurred first in the Divine Mind where ideas of less and lack and their opposites do not exist. The infinite Divine Mind perceives everything in perfection and completeness, beyond duality, ever present and without the limitations of time, space, and dimensions.

Even if everyone on earth understood how to manifest a pink Cadillac and everyone received a car, the infinite storehouse of the universe could still provide a car for everyone who wanted two or three or more. You can have as many as you want. It simply requires you thinking a consecutive thought that is sustained over time.

SEEING BEYOND ERROR

Appearances of things (for example, disease) can produce an idea in the mind and it will manifest in the body. But if you know the truth—for example, that health, not disease, is the true reality—then you can let go of the appearance and embrace the truth. This is an important concept for those who want financial prosperity but see the absence of wealth and consider poverty to be the truth. The fear of disease can cause it to manifest, but a focus on health can bestow vitality. Fear of poverty can impede finding wealth, but a focus on abundance can draw prosperity.

Christian Scientists—not to be confused with Scientologists or material or physical scientists—are guided by the principle that the spiritual reality is the only real truth and all else is spiritual error. That is why they believe they can heal through the power of prayer. When a person's faith is strong enough to see the body's illness as no more than an illusion or a spiritual error in the mind, that faith restores perfection and wholeness. This is another important truth to be shared with others who desire to work with the Law of Attraction to attract optimum health.

EMPOWER OTHERS

Every person comes up against limits throughout life. Assuming that each person has a God-given mind for reasoning, a heart for feeling, and a healthy and whole body for getting through life, what makes one person able to push past limitations to become a magnet for the things they desire while the other person fails? Someone who struggles with lack most likely experiences one or more of the following limiting habits: inability to focus, lack of imagination, tendency to procrastinate, doubt, judgmental and critical self-talk, fear, and self-limiting beliefs.

FIND THE GOOD

Empower others everywhere you go. Do as the late Alex Haley, the author of *Roots*, advocated: "Find the good and praise it." Celebrate life and let your enthusiasm for doing and seeing good be a lightning rod for others, so that they will desire to live in that kind of happiness. Remind yourself and others that in every moment is the power to change the course of your day or your life. The miracles that go on around us—miracles we often don't even notice—are manifestations of the law at work in the world. Now that's a reassurance to celebrate!

MOVING BEYOND SELF-LIMITATIONS

You can encourage others to recognize the negativity in their thoughts and behaviors. Since they alone own them, they must be the ones who shift the paradigm. By choosing to break the destructive cycles of negative thoughts, words, and actions and to move into alignment with positive and happy thinking, feeling, doing, and speaking, they become empowered to move beyond the appearances of limitations.

Energy, Enthusiasm, and Expectation

Not surprisingly, many people working with deliberate intention and the Law of Attraction have sought and found support among others who share their ideas about how to achieve the good things in life. The group energy and enthusiasm is often infectious and spurs individuals in the group to believe in the value of their dreams and let go of doubt and the negatives of the past that may weigh upon them.

Sometimes members of a Law of Attraction networking group will help you clarify and establish goals or work toward new ones. You, in turn, help them stay on track. The group can help you identify behaviors that may create luck in bringing success or factors that may be chasing it away. You reinforce one another's pursuit of goodness, not just the acquisition of material wealth but in the expectation that your sacred dreams, your goals of working with service groups, and your humanitarian efforts will come to fruition.

CHALLENGING THE STATUS QUO

People who are successful in creating their exciting dream life are always on the move. They don't sit still and wait for life to come to them. They won't write one book in a year; they'll write two, four, or five. They won't start just one business in a lifetime. They will build one until it becomes mega-successful, and then they'll begin again with something new. They sail into life each day with zeal and gusto, ever on the lookout for a new idea, a more fun way to do something, or a new enterprise, ever challenging the status quo. By demonstrating that passionate way of being, you are demonstrating how to best work with the law. You may be motivating yourself as well.

LEARNING METAPHYSICAL AND ESOTERIC TEACHINGS

Some Law of Attraction practitioners join support groups to share metaphysical or esoteric teachings behind the Law of Attraction. Others are attracted to the open and honest ways that members engage in self-disclosure and friendship. They no longer feel isolated in the pursuit of a new and better life. Still others find that it helps to work with fellow Buddhists or survivors of some life-threatening disease who support one another through several layers of common interest, such as a desire for compassionate living or a sense of shared common ground.

SHOWING OTHERS HOW TO CREATE A NEW LIFE

Some Law of Attraction teachers talk about how to get everything you want from positive thinking. They expound on various points that they believe are key to becoming an attraction magnet for abundance of every kind. Many people will remain skeptical and won't believe it is possible to create such a life until they see someone else do it. Show them how to create a good life, centered in thanksgiving and gratitude. Inspire others to become self-reliant and independent.

KEY POINTS

When sharing information that is critical to working with the law, it is helpful to emphasize that the most successful individuals refuse to settle for mediocrity in life. They see change as exciting and necessary. In fact, they create it when they form intention for their new life of prosperity and joy. They don't just desire something; they go after it with a passion. They let go of old paradigms and patterns that did not bring successful results.

Another key point to emphasize is the importance of persistence, not only in formulating the belief that a goal is worthwhile but in continuing to believe that the goal can be reached. Further, it is critical that an individual who is starting to work with the law firmly believes that he is worthy of the goals and desires he sets forth to achieve. He must have the persistence of Henry Ford, whose engineers at first did not believe it was possible to create a six-cylinder motor, and hold on to his vision passionately despite the naysayers.

TAKING THE LAW WHERE IT IS MOST NEEDED

Some critics have suggested that those who have most passionately rallied behind the Law of Attraction are members of America's middle class. But the people who really need the hope promised by the law are poor people, the hungry, those living in shelters and on the streets, and the disenfranchised. The teachings of Jesus found resonance with just such groups because their society 2,000 years ago failed them.

HELP A YOUNGER GENERATION

Young people today face many of the same challenges of growing up as those of previous generations but, in addition, must find ways to deal with media messages that glorify negative patterns of thinking and living. Gangsta rap and some hip-hop lyrics glorify gang life and romanticize infidelity, promiscuity, abuse, hatred, and drug use. America's prisons are full of young people who associated with the wrong peer group.

Who are the positive role models for today's youth? More often, the tabloids and TV shows run stories of such individuals entering or leaving rehab, partying endlessly, or showing off a destructive lifestyle with an emphasis on sensual indulgence and disregard for the rule of law.

Teachers, youth counselors, parents, and peers could do more to help the younger generation relate to better role models, to celebrate their success as if it were their own, to promote their interests as if they were self-serving interests. It's a radical concept to teach young people, but if they can conceive that all of humanity is interconnected on some level and that one act of goodness affects everyone, perhaps they would be inspired to live noble lives.

COUNSELING YOUNG ADULTS

Surely it could greatly benefit young people to learn about how they can create a positive and meaningful life for themselves. A self-centered, decadent lifestyle that leaves one burned out by the age of thirty does not benefit the individual, the family, the community, or society at large. Begin to reach out to young people, at first your own, to give them the tools to go after their dreams. Remind them that it is possible to change the world one person at a time and that making the world a better place for everyone, including future generations, is an admirable goal.

Many teens tune out adult guidance as they push up against the boundaries of their world as part of their biological task to individuate away from the family. But they listen to each other. One of the best ways to get across a message of hope is to let the teens spread it among themselves. Just imagine how such teaching might help someone scared and confused and ready to give up completely on her life.

Offer to participate in career day at your local high school. Use that venue to discuss how the Law of Attraction helped you find the right job, get promoted, start your own company, or further your career. Show genuine passion and enthusiasm for your work and your life to inspire your young audience. Use concrete examples from your life.

CREATING HIGH-QUALITY GOLDEN YEARS

Senior citizens represent a sector of the population who could use knowledge of the Law of Attraction. They are often vulnerable, sometimes suffering more than others from a lack of money, health care coverage, affordable medications, and sometimes even food and housing. Sharing techniques and strategies for intentionally working with the Law of Attraction might help members of the aging population create not only longer and healthier lives, but a better quality of life. While they may not have the energy or the same dreams they had in their youth, some may still hope to find a pot of gold at the end of the rainbow and likely would share it with others.

Through the sharing of your experience of intentionally working with the Law of Attraction, remember to include a discussion of the roles of faith and gratitude. Teaching others about the law so that they might have better lives, greater happiness, and a more prosperous future has resonance in the Buddhist idea of humanity's interconnectedness and the necessity of each person to have a sense of responsibility toward the welfare of others. In Buddhism, the highest ideal is the path of the bodhisattva. The bodhisattva finds the source of all fulfillment—that is, the Ultimate Truth—but he denies himself enlightenment in order to bring all other fellow beings to that same holy Source.

CHAPTER 6

What's Next?

A BRIGHTER FUTURE

Consider how you might envision ways of attracting to you the means to help others build a better and brighter future. Consider how you could use your powerful and magnetized thoughts to bring about change in your community, country, and the world. Some say the Berlin Wall came down through the prayers of the world and the inspiration of then-President Ronald Reagan saying, "Mr. Gorbachev, tear down this wall."

WHO ELSE WOULD YOU HELP?

As you previously learned, you can't change another human being, but you can choose to behave differently around that person, and that is enough to shift the dynamics of a relationship with her. If you are in a bad relationship, dissatisfied with your employer, or have reached the end of your patience with a disgruntled client, you can choose to sever the connection and go in a different direction in your life. Bless those individuals as you move forward. But why not also see them bathed in holy light in your mind and silently bless them so that they may have the highest good that can come to them? Ask yourself, "Who else might benefit from my knowledge of how to work with the Law of Attraction?"

WORK TOWARD OPEN DOORS

Perhaps one of the most important things the late mythologist Joseph Campbell said was to follow your bliss. What if you were at a crossroads in your life, feeling like you didn't know which way to turn? Maybe a door has closed on your marriage or career. Perhaps now the time is right to visit Italy or France, set up your software business in Ireland, start your import store on eBay, or establish an orphanage in India. If those ideas seem too grand, consider doing some volunteer work at home or abroad. Use the Law of Attraction to draw in those doors that Campbell said will open as you follow your bliss. As they do swing open, confidently walk through them. Just as the law has drawn a door closed, it will open others and help you across the threshold.

FIND YOUR JOY

Are you someone who laughs easily at the craziness of life? You have already learned how important emotion is in magnetizing thought. Find your inner child and laugh often with his childhood delight as you move into your new life of working with the Law of Attraction. You'll find that humor helps defuse tense situations, adds levity to the most serious moments, and ensures that you never take yourself (or anyone else, for that matter) too seriously.

MATERIAL OR SPIRITUAL GAIN?

The Law of Attraction is available to all. But some people practice working with it more than others. You might choose to make an in-depth study of its working in your life and the lives of others. Consider disseminating your knowledge and experience in working with the law. Teach seminars, write a newsletter, direct a conference, produce a video or CD, or establish a website devoted to the Law of Attraction. From your work and special expertise and insights, you could charge fees that could become an income stream, perhaps the means of helping yourself get out of debt or begin to build wealth. Doing such work with a sense of high-minded purpose, not greed, makes it noble. However, you might also decide that you want to help others who are less fortunate and pursue Law of Attraction work as a purely spiritual endeavor. When you are motivated by selflessness to do good for others, your activities generate spiritual dividends.

COLLECTIVE ENVISIONING FOR GLOBAL CHANGE

Consider how you join in with others working with the Law of Attraction to build a better world. With them, you would need to be unified in purpose, hold the same collective vision and intentions, and make a deep emotional commitment to imagine a world without war, leaders coming up with solutions to global social ills, and corporations becoming good citizens and responsible stewards of the planet. Perhaps you and your group could focus on the eradication of hunger, cures for HIV/AIDS and cancer, abolition of racism and bigotry, or other issues.

What Is the Gaia Philosophy?

Gaia is a name used within the green community and in certain scientific circles to explain the concept that all the living organisms of a host planet cooperate with their environment to function as a single self-regulating system. In Greek mythology, Gaia was the goddess of the earth.

POSITIVE THINKING FOR THE PLANET

Think of yourself as one member of a global family who works with the Law of Attraction to envision the well-being of planet Earth. Many people, not just those who embrace the Gaia philosophy, are persuaded that much has to be done to reduce the human footprint, not only on earth but in the heavens.

TRANSFORMATIONAL THINKING THAT GOES BEYOND PERSONAL DREAMS AND GOALS

As you begin to manifest helpful people, wonderful relationships, and the things you've always wanted, begin to think outside the box in radical new ways. Try envisioning new life goals, determining a new purpose or career path, or projecting new plans for a business or organization.

USE THE LAW IN YOUR PLACE OF WORSHIP

Use the Law of Attraction in your place of worship to achieve fundraising goals, restore the building, buy new materials, expand outreach programs, envision a return to health for the sick . . . and in myriad other ways. Share ideas about positive thinking and how to work with the Law of Attraction with fellow parishioners.

USE THE LAW TO BRING ABOUT ECOLOGICAL AND ENVIRONMENTAL CHANGES

You can join with others to dream a grand dream of ecological and environmental change. Develop affirmations for group recitation. Prepare and implement to-do or action lists that might include calling upon government representatives to ensure environmentally friendly products, good alternatives to fossil fuels, safer food supplies through reduction of harmful pesticides and hormone injections of animals, responsible e-waste recycling, preservation of the rain forests, and safer water supplies.

MIND AND BODY CONTROL FOR PERFECT HEALTH

By using the Law of Attraction, you can manifest perfect mental and physical health. Using the power of your mind you can bring about healthy changes in your body, even overcome the kinds of diseases that can shorten your life. Life extension is certainly possible through an understanding of dietary rules, exercising, stress reduction, smoking cessation, moderate consumption of coffee and alcohol, and deliberate work to manifest perfect health in harmony with the Law of Attraction.

Some Indian yogis have been able to slow their heartbeat and breathing in order to demonstrate mental power over their bodies. Stories that defy human logic and understanding have circulated. People have even been buried alive, slept on pallets of pointed nails, or pulled a heavy object using hooks in the skin of their backs. Still others were able to know things about total strangers or the nature and composition of a certain object. Sathya Sai Baba, a controversial Hindu holy man born in the Indian village of Puttaparthi, can manifest things out of the air by the power of his thought. He has done hundreds of demonstrations throughout his lifetime and is considered by millions to be an avatar or incarnation of God. When he materializes things such as gems and sacred ash, he is said to chant "It is coming now." That phrase, spoken with resolve and faith, is an excellent one to use when working with the Law of Attraction.

Think of other examples of what you could manifest in your life. For example, you might manifest approval, love, higher ethical standards, understanding, insight, acceptance, hopefulness, peace, agility, strength, purpose, tenderness, fearlessness, veracity, confidence, a winning spirit, deep spiritual insights, and exceptional competence.

AWAKENING POWERFUL ENERGY CENTERS

Your body contains two extremely powerful energy centers, the heart and the crown chakras (among others). Your destiny—and that of everyone, some say—is to be transformed into spiritually evolved beings. That happens through the awakening and ascent of the kundalini energy up through the spinal channel known as the *sushumna*. Kundalini is the divine transformational energy that can bestow knowledge of the past and future, the mysteries of the universe, and the secrets of all creation when it is activated or awakened.

GETTING STARTED

The Law of Attraction will bring you what you deeply desire and need. If you need a teacher to help you on your spiritual path, you have only to ask for one. There's an old adage that states that when the student is ready, the teacher appears.

Your greatest benefit of an awakened kundalini is the culmination of the process of spiritual maturation. Kundalini arousal can bring about self-realization or the recognition of the atman, knowledge of the true self. Some say it confers immortality.

Some yogis and yoginis say that you can attract the conditions for the awakening of the kundalini through mantra, mudra, breath work, meditation, and other spiritual practices. The kundalini awakening can occur spontaneously or through *shaktipat*, the transference of energy from a teacher to a student for the purpose of initiation and awakening of the kundalini. Such awakening confers powers from all the energy centers of the body and brings about superconsciousness.

Your Energy Awaits

The Sanskrit meaning of kundalini is "coiled up." Yogis believe that at the base of the spine, a latent divine energy awaits awakening. Usually depicted in religious or spiritual literature and imagery as a coiled serpent, it is wrapped around itself three and one-half times.

You may feel pressure, especially at the base of the spine, a column of heat from the tailbone to the top of the head, sounds such as tinkling bells or thunder, the sensation of ants crawling along the spine, the sound of the cosmic vibration of atoms heard as "Om," and cool and hot energy flowing along the spinal column. These are just some of the signs and symptoms. Others have heard bees buzzing and seen (through the third-eye chakra) streams of light. In India, some practitioners of yoga have found themselves spontaneously doing certain yoga poses or mudras (hand positions).

LIVING YOUR LIFE INSIDE OUT

Kundalini Shakti is perceived as a manifestation of the energetic feminine form of the Divine. When you decide to seek a higher spiritual life and begin to attract wisdom and spiritual understanding instead of "stuff," she will begin to open and empower the energy centers of the body, according to the teachings of Kundalini Maha yoga. You will become transformed. Instead of living in a material world and having your body senses dictating how you live your life, you can choose to live out your days in a different way—from the inside out.

ETERNAL NOW

When your heart is open and your mind is beyond dualistic thinking, you can truly live in the present moment with consciousness of all moments—past, present, and future—contained in one time/space continuum. Yogis say that for such holy beings, there is nothing that can't be known or done.

The purpose of life, some believe, is self-development and the unfolding of the divine latent powers within. In *The Seven Spiritual Laws of Success,* Dr. Deepak Chopra references the Law of Pure Potentiality, also known as the Law of Unity (because underlying infinite diversity is the unity of the One). These are universal laws, just like the Law of Attraction. As you dream this dream of your life, you tap into the realm of infinite possibility. It isn't to be found outside of you, but rather within.

INFINITE POSSIBILITIES

The Law of Karma will bring experiences into your life as you consciously and unconsciously send out your thoughts, but you get to decide how to handle what comes. Imagine the possibilities of always knowing the right thing to do and the right moment in which to do it. Consider being able to block illness from ever coming into your body, or to attract unfathomable wealth. Imagine being able to traverse the cosmos by imagery and thought. Think about how you might use infinite power and wisdom for peace and other high and noble purposes. You have the power to transform yourself into a self-realized or enlightened being. In fact, an Indian sage named Patanjali wrote a book to explain how, *The Yoga Sutras.*

When you desire enlightenment, the power switch is flipped on, and light dispels darkness or ignorance. Your usual state of being becomes one of peace and joy or bliss. Enlightened, you possess the kingdom of God, for in the state of self-realization, you become godlike. According to some yogis, god-realized individuals know all that is knowable, and even if the sacred texts from all religious paths were destroyed, a god-realized being could recreate them. People won't recognize you by all the "stuff" you have attracted and manifested, but rather by your expression of love, wisdom, and power. Find the secret hidden deep inside your heart. As Rumi, the Sufi mystic might say, someone is calling you; maybe it's your own soul asking you to open the door.

Glossary

affirmations
Positive statements that are repeated to impress and reinforce a particular belief.

aphorism
A succinct saying that embodies a truth—for example, the aphorisms of Patanjali's *The Yoga Sutras*.

Ayurveda
The ancient Hindu art of medicine that emphasizes the vital energies of the body as well as knowledge of prolonging life.

covenant
The promises made by God to humans that are found in the Scriptures.

Creator
One of many monikers for God; others include Divine Intelligence, Holy One, Divine Mind, Power(s) that Be, the Universe, and the Nameless Formless One; the aspect of the omnipotent, omniscient, and omnipresent God that brought and brings all things into being.

dowsing
The method by which a pendulum or forked stick is used to detect energies from the earth or environment as a means of finding water or divining information.

dharma
A way of living in which a person strives to have in perfect alignment his or her body, mind, and spirit.

Emerald Tablet

A tablet discovered by archeologists with verses attributed to Hermes Trismegistus.

emotion

The mood created by positive or negative feelings in the body in response to internal or external stimulus.

feng shui

The ancient Chinese art of placement and energy flow.

Kabbalah (also Cabala, Qabalah)

The practices and texts of Jewish mystical teachings that were developed by rabbis from the seventh to the eighteenth centuries. Initiates interpreted sacred Scripture through insights that allowed them to foretell the future. Kabbalah reached its zenith, perhaps, in the medieval period to the Renaissance.

kami

In the animist Shinto religion, kami represents a divine force or being that may be found in rock formations or along rivers and in mountains.

karma

The Hindu philosophy of retribution in the current life of an individual attributed to his or her past thoughts, words, or actions.

Kundalini Shakti

The latent divine energy in the subtle (spiritual) body that, according to ancient Vedic philosophy, awakens spontaneously or through initiation by a teacher to move up the pathway along the spine to the top of the head to confer union with Divine consciousness.

mudra

Movement of the hands in yoga positions, meditation, or classical Indian dance, the latter as a way of expressing feeling.

Om (also Aum)

In Hinduism, regarded as the sound that is a complete expression of the Divine in that it encompasses Brahma (the Creator), Vishnu (Preserver), and Shiva (the Destroyer); also the primordial sound of vibratory creation.

Patanjali

A sage in the tradition of Vedic Hinduism who collected verses known as sutras or aphorisms that expounded the philosophy of the raja yoga path to enlightenment.

pendulum

A device, such as a crystal suspended from a chain and bead, used to detect energy (often water) sources or to divine information.

prana

In yoga, one of five vital breaths.

psychic energy

A mental energy that can be detected and utilized in certain psychological activities.

sadhana

Spiritual practices aimed at helping a soul advance toward enlightenment.

sushumna

The channel of the subtle body that in Vedic philosophy connects the chakra, or energy center, at the base of the spine with the crown chakra on the top of the head and through which the sacred kundalini rises.

tarot

Cards used for divination; fortune-telling cards that originated during medieval times.

transformational thinking

Radical new ways of thinking that create a shift in consciousness.

universal laws

Various forces at work in the universe that conform to given behaviors under specific circumstances but not, however, necessarily recognized by orthodox science as provable.

visualization

The act of intentionally creating images in the mind through use of the imagination.

APPENDIX B

Resources

The following books may prove to be excellent resources for rounding out your knowledge of various disciplines that tie into a fuller understanding of deliberately working with the Law of Attraction.

Barrett, Jayme. *Feng Shui Your Life*. Second Edition. New York: Sterling Publications, 2012.

Bruce-Mitford, Miranda. *Signs and Symbols*. DK Publishing, 2008.

Byrne, Rhonda. *The Secret*. New York: Atria Books, 2006.

Chopra, Deepak. *The Seven Spiritual Laws of Success*. Novato, CA: Amber-Allen/New World, 1994.

Csikszentmihalyi, Mihaly. *Flow: The Psychology of Optimal Experience*. New York: Harper Perennial, 1991.

Eason, Cassandra. *The Art of the Pendulum*. Boston: Weiser Books, 2005.

Ellerman, David. *Helping People Help Themselves: From the World Bank to an Alternative Philosophy of Development Assistance*. Ann Arbor: University of Michigan Press, 2006.

Gimbutas, Marija. *The Language of the Goddess*. New York: Harper & Row, 2001.

Goldwell, Bruce and Tammy Lynch. *Mastery of Abundant Living: The Key to Mastering the Law of Attraction*. Calgary: Saga Books, 2007.

Hicks, Ester and Jerry. *Ask and It Is Given: Learning to Manifest Your Desires*. Carlsbad: Hay House, 2009.

Hicks, Esther and Jerry. *The Law of Attraction: The Basics of the Teachings of Abraham*. Carlsbad: Hay House, 2006.

Hill, Napoleon. *Think and Grow Rich*. New York: Tarcher, 2005.

L'Engle, Madeleine. *Walking on Water: Reflections on Faith and Art*. Colorado Springs, CO: Shaw Books, 2001.

Losier, Michael J. *The Law of Attraction, The Science of Attracting More of What You Want and Less of What You Don't*. New York: Wellness Central, 2007.

O'Connor, Cathleen. *The Everything® Law of Attraction Dream Dictionary*. Avon: Adams Media, 2012.

Peale, Norman Vincent. *The Power of Positive Thinking*. New York: Fireside, 2003.

Ray, James Arthur. *The Science of Success: How to Attract Prosperity and Create Harmonic Wealth Through Proven Principles*. Carlsbad, CA: Sun Ark Press, 1999.

Stasney, Sharon. *Feng Shui Living*. New York: Sterling Publications, 2003.

Walker, Barbara. *The Woman's Dictionary of Symbols and Sacred Objects*. San Francisco: Harper & Row, 1983.

Wattles, Wallace D. *The Science of Getting Rich: Financial Success Through Creative Thought*. New York: Barnes & Noble, 2007.

Weil, Andrew. *8 Weeks to Optimum Health, New Edition, Expanded and Updated: A Proven Program for Taking Full Advantage of Your Body's Natural Healing Power*. New York: Time Warner Paperbacks (New Ed.), 2007.

Weil, Andrew. *Spontaneous Healing: How to Discover and Embrace Your Body's Natural Ability to Maintain and Heal Itself*. New York: Ballantine, 2000.

WEB SOURCES

About.com, Alternative Religious Symbols
http://altreligion.about.com/od/symbols/tp/symbols_guide.htm

Center for Consciousness Studies
www.consciousness.Arizona.edu/mission.htm

Dr.Weil.com
www.drweil.com

Hinduism Today
www.hinduismtoday.com

International Association for the Study of Dreams
www.asdreams.org

Jean Houston
www.jeanhouston.org

The Mary Baker Eddy Library
www.marybakereddylibrary.org

New Thought Library
www.newthoughtlibrary.com

Rupert Sheldrake
www.sheldrake.org

Index